Emotional Intelligence 2.0

A Guide to Manage Anger, Overcome Negativity and Master your Emotions

Shanice Johnson

Contents

INTRODUCTION

Recently, it seems like the world is being submerged in so much negativity to the point where it is almost impossible to avoid being drenched by this rain of negativity. There is just so much strife, stress, anxiety, sadness, dissatisfaction, and anger ruining humans. This has made many people turn to self-development as a means of escaping the negativity hovering around. However, try as they may, they seem to find no resource, book, or person to teach them what they really want to know which is: how to overcome negativity and embrace positivity successfully.

If you are currently reading this, it means you are one of the people striving so hard to get rid of anger, stress, and anxiety in order to build a life of positivity for themselves. Well, count yourself lucky because you have just found your one-stop-shop to everything you need to know about anger, stress, and anxiety management; you can now find out everything you need to know about overcoming negativity. These pages contain genuine information, tips, strategies, and techniques that can help you create that happy, negativity-devoid, and quality life you desire and as well, deserve.

The book is written in simplified and easy-to-digest language to help you assimilate everything contained within smoothly.

Reading "Emotional Intelligence – A Guide to Manage Anger, Overcome Negativity and Master your Emotions" opens your mind to a stress-free life filled with positivity, productivity, and purpose. The book will teach you all you need to know about stress management, anxiety management, and anger management by making you privy to some of the most effective techniques and strategies for mastering your emotions and learning emotional intelligence. It will begin by explaining all the basics you need to know about emotions; the nature of emotions; and the sources of emotions. What impacts our emotions? How are emotions developed? Are negative emotions even necessary at all? How can you get rid of them? These and many more are the questions you will be finding valid answers to in "Emotional Intelligence – A Guide to Manage Anger, Overcome Negativity and Master your Emotions."

We will also take an in-depth look at what emotional intelligence 2.0 is and how it can help you rid your life of negativity. Most importantly, you will learn about anger management and core relaxation strategies to get rid of worries, concerns, and uncertainties. To further help you, we will be giving you tips on how to practice mindfulness meditation which is a popular form of meditation now being used to practice self-awareness. Mindfulness meditation technique can help you develop your connection with your inner self so that you can develop high emotional intelligence.

If you are interested in leading a value-laden life, qualitative, and filled with positivity; if you want to learn to project positivity into negative emotions and you would like to learn how you can be more productive, purposeful, and positive in life but you don't know where to begin from, this one-stop-shop for positivity promises to teach you these and everything else you need to know. Every answer you need awaits you in this amazing read.

The choice is now left to you to choose a life devoid of stress, anger, anxiety; a life of positivity; and start living life with a de-cluttered and free mind using the strategies, tips, and techniques waiting for you in the book.

CHAPTER ONE

WHAT ARE EMOTIONS?

Understanding the nature of emotions and what emotions are is the first step to learning how to successfully master your emotions. After all, how could you master something if you don't even know what it is or how it works? According to the dictionary, emotions can be defined as "a person's internal state of being and involuntary physiological response to an object or a situation, based on or tied to physical state and sensory data." In a simpler definition, the Oxford dictionary says emotion is "a strong feeling deriving from one's circumstances, mood, or relationships with others." From both definitions, you can already tell that those emotions are related to feelings in a certain way. However, emotions and feelings are not entirely the same. Human emotions are usually triggered by changes in a person's physiological and behavioral makeup.

As humans, we can usually tell our emotional state at every point. You know when you are feeling happy, sad, or angry. However, what you cannot probably tell is where exactly these feelings originate from. Usually, most of us make the mistake of regarding emotions and feelings as the same thing. We even use both interchangeably in the form of synonyms. But, as we have said; emotions and feelings are two different things that are somehow dependent on each other. While emotions originate from a subconscious and physiological state, feelings are mostly subjective to experiences, and they originate from a conscious state. Emotions may be regarded as automatic bodily reactions to internal or external triggers. Therefore, we can say that there may be emotions without feelings but there can be no feelings without emotions. Feelings are subjects of our emotional state.

Every emotion humans experience has four important components which are: cognitive, behavioral, physiological and affective reactions. When you experience an emotion, it is usually triggered and fueled by either of these four components.

Firstly, cognitive reaction to emotions refers to how a person thinks, stores information and experiences, and perceives an event. Behavioral reactions have to do with how humans primarily express an emotion. Physiological reactions, on the other hand, are triggered by changes in a person's hormonal level. Finally, affect reaction signify the state of emotion and the nature of the emotion itself. Each aspect of emotions as explained usually triggers the other. For instance, let's say that an aunt you don't like comes to visit your parents; immediately you see this person, you automatically think in your mind that she is annoying or scary probably due to past experiences with her and her disposition (this is a cognitive reaction). Due to this perception you have of your annoying aunt, you become grumpy (this is the affect reaction). Then, your parents come to tell you that your aunt will be staying in the house for a while; you feel your blood rising in anger (this is a physiological reaction) and you angrily leave for your room (behavioral reaction). To understand the different components of emotions, you must ensure you know where emotions originate from. Experts have tried to identify the source of emotions using different theories. These theories try to explain the processes of emotions formulation, the sources of emotions, and the cause. We will be looking into these theories, although not in-depth. We will try to understand how emotions occur solitary.

In the bid to explain emotions, researchers have formulated different theories which are classified under three main categories. We have the physiological theories which propose that emotions are the results of certain responses to the body; there are the neurological theories which suggest that certain activities that take place in the brain are responsible for our emotions; finally, there are theories under the cognitive class which believe that our thoughts, perceptions, and mental activities are responsible for the formulation of emotions.

The first theory that tries to explain emotions is the "evolutionary theory of emotion" which was proposed by Charles Darwin, a naturalist. This theory argues that emotions evolve due to their adaptive nature which promotes human survival and reproduction. Darwin also said that humans seek to reproduce with mates due to feelings of love and affection which are products of feelings. He further explained that feelings of fear cause people to recognize and flee from danger. According to Darwin, we have emotions because we need them to adapt and survive in whatever environment we find ourselves. Emotions trigger appropriate responses to certain stimuli in the environment, thereby promoting our chances of survival. To survive in any environment, we have to be cognizant of our own emotions and that of others. However, it is not enough to be aware of emotions, we must also be able to interpret, control, and respond appropriately to a trigger. Being able to correctly interpret our emotions and that of others makes it possible for us to give suitable and appropriate responses to any situation we find ourselves.

Next is the James-Lange theory which is a prominent physiological theory of emotion. This theory was proposed individually by Carl Lange, a physiologist, and William James, a psychologist. The James-Lange theory of emotion argues that emotions are bodily responses which are triggered as a result of the body's physiological reactions to certain events. According to James and Lange, the emotions you produce in response to a physiological reaction caused by a stimulus in the environment is dependent on your interpretation of the physiological reaction. For instance, if you are watching a frightening scene in a movie and you feel your heart start to the race, James and Lange believe that you will interpret the physiological reaction (of your heart racing) as you being scared. Then, you conclude that you are frightened since your heart is racing. The James-Lange physiological theory of emotion proposes that your heart isn't racing because you are scared; rather, you are scared because your heart is racing. Therefore, the emotion of fear you are feeling then is a response to the physiological reaction taking place in your body.

Another prominent theory that seeks to explain the origin and nature of emotions is the Cannon-Bard theory of emotion. This is also a physiological theory but it seeks to directly counter the submissions of James and Lange. Proposed by Walter Cannon and further expanded by Philip Bard, this theory explains that humans experience physiological reactions linked to certain emotions without necessarily experiencing these emotions. For example, your heart also races when you do something exciting such as exercise, not just when you are scared. According to Cannon, people experience emotional responses so quickly that they simply can't be the result of some physical reactions. As an example, when you watch that frightening movie scene, you often start to feel scared even before noticing that your heart is racing or your hands are trembling. Cannon and Bard, in essence, argue that emotional responses and physiological reactions often occur simultaneously to internal or external stimuli.

The Schachter-Singer theory is another theory of emotion which examines emotions from a cognitive perspective. According to this theory, humans first experience a physiological reaction after which they try to identify the cause of this reaction so they can experience it as an emotion. In other words, you react to external or internal stimuli with a physiological response which you then interpret from a cognitive perspective; the result of the cognitive interpretation is what is considered an emotion. The Schachter and Singer theory is quite similar to both James-Lange and Cannon-Bard's theory but the main difference is the cognitive interpretation which humans use to label an emotion, according to Schachter and Singer. Like Cannon and Bard, Schachter and Singer also argued that certain physiological responses in the body can result in different emotions.

The Lazarus theory of emotion or Cognitive Appraisal theory as it is also called was proposed by Richard Lazarus and is another theory that takes a cognitive approach. This theory suggests that thinking always takes place before emotion is experienced. According to Lazarus and other pioneers of this theory, humans react to stimuli immediately with thoughts, after which the physiological response and emotions are experienced. This means that your thoughts always come first before a physiological and emotional response. For example, if you are watching a frightening scene of a movie, your mind immediately starts to think that this movie is scary and frightening. This triggers an emotion of fear, accompanied by related physical reactions such as hands trembling, racing heart, etc.

Finally, we have the Facial-Feedback theory of emotion. This theory suggests that emotional experiences are linked to our facial expressions. What this means is that your physical reactions to stimuli have a direct impact on the emotion you experience, instead of being the effects of the emotion. This theory argues that our emotions are directly linked to changes in our facial muscles. For instance, if you force yourself to smile more when interacting with people, you will have a better time at social events. And, if you carry a frown whenever you interact with people at social events, you had feel an awful emotion.

These are all theories of emotions which experts have proposed over the years. You may wonder why you even need to learn about the theories of emotions just because you want to learn how to control your emotions. To master your emotions, there is one key thing you must first do; understand how emotions occur. If you want to learn to control an emotion like anger, you need to first identify the source of the anger and all the symptoms associated with it. Once you know this, you can easily put a leash on your rage the next time you feel it brewing.

Emotions are an important part of our lives because they have huge impacts on our actions, reactions, decisions, and ultimately, our lives. There may still be a huge cloud of mystery surrounding why humans experience emotions but with the little knowledge available to us, we should be able to understand and manage our emotions effectively.

EMOTIONAL INTELLIGENCE: WHAT EXACTLY IS IT?

While you may know what emotional intelligence is due to the buzz it has been getting recently, you probably don't understand what it is to a maximum extent. Many of us hear all about emotional intelligence and how it is so important but we don't quite understand what exactly it is about and why it seems to be so important. Well, emotional intelligence is the same as mastering your emotions; you can, in fact, use the two interchangeably in a conversation. However, emotional intelligence goes beyond the scope of mastering your own emotions; it extends far into being able to master the emotions of others too. You are probably wondering how that is even possible right now but it is.

In clear terms, emotional intelligence is regarded as the ability to understand, manage, use, and control your own emotions and that of others in a way that helps you achieve positive results. Without emotional intelligence, it would be impossible for you to master and manage your emotions to improve the quality of your life and your relationship with others. Emotional intelligence has four key aspects which are: self-awareness, self-management, social awareness, and relationship management.

Self-awareness has to do with being able to recognize and identify your emotions and how they influence your thoughts and behaviors. It has to do with being cognizant of your emotional state at all times and being able to manage this emotional state so that it doesn't negatively impact your actions, decisions, and reactions towards others. When you are self-aware, you recognize your strengths, weaknesses, and preferences. You can tell what kind of conversations get your blood boiling in rage and which ones make your heart race and excite you about the future. Being cognizant of one's emotions makes it easier to manage these emotions and control how they affect our lives.

Self-management is another key aspect of emotional intelligence which has to do with being able to control and manage impulses, feelings, and behaviors which are all triggers of emotions. The ability to self-manage means you can put impulsive feelings and thoughts under control and avoid them leading you to make rash decisions. For instance, good self-management is when you walk away from the scene after someone hits you instead of hitting them back. Of course, when someone hits you, there is a rush of anger that leads to an impulse to hit this person back, probably even harder. But when you drive this impulse under control without giving in to it, this is what self-management is.

Social awareness is another key aspect of mastering emotional intelligence and it is the ability to empathize with others. A person who is socially aware can understand the emotions of other people, recognize emotional cues, and feel concerns for the needs of others. Being socially aware means you are able to perceive another person's emotions or needs even before they voice out and you take the cue to respond with an appropriate reaction fitting to the emotion. For example, when you are socially aware, you know the right thing to say to make someone happy; you don't get someone angry when you intend to make them happy. This is particularly key to having important social interactions with people. Finally, the relationship management aspect of emotional intelligence involves a person's ability to build and manage positive relationships with others. It is the ability to have good communications with others in a way that you can easily influence and inspire their actions, reactions, and behaviors towards you.

At first thought, you may not fully understand the importance of emotional intelligence. But, with further thinking and perception, you will realize that emotional intelligence has a huge impact on your personal and professional life. Emotional intelligence directly impacts your career, mental and physical health, relationships, and social intelligence. To master your emotions, you must develop self-cognizance and self-management. Once you do this, it becomes easier to build and maintain social relationships.

The ability to understand your emotions and manage them is fundamental to overcoming negativity and leading a life of positivity. As humans, we have been created to be very emotional and social beings. So, it is quite easy for us to allow our emotions to interfere with our social life. Without mastering your emotions, becoming a high-functioning human with a quality life is almost impossible. Therefore, striving to become emotionally intelligent will teach you to create a balance between your personal life and your relationship with others. It will help you achieve success in basically every aspect of your life.

Once you can identify, understand, and manage your positive and negative emotions effectively, you can easily control anxiety, stress, anger and other negativities which poorly impact the quality of your relationships. Next, let's look at the different types of emotions, both negative and positive. Knowing and understanding the different types of emotions and the category they fall under advances your chances of effective emotion mastering.

DIFFERENT TYPES OF EMOTIONS: NEGATIVE AND POSITIVE

Emotions can usually be categorized into two different types. However, these types come in different forms. Some experts categorize emotions into two types: emotions to be expressed and emotions to be controlled. Others categorize emotions as primary emotions and secondary emotions. However, is all kinds of emotions are usually either positive or negative. Whether emotion is primary/secondary or expressed/controlled, it will either be negative or positive. Often, people believe that positive psychology is centered mainly on positive emotions but this isn't quite true. In truth, positive psychology leans more towards negative emotions because it is more about managing and overturning negative emotions to achieve positive results.

Firstly, positive emotions may be defined as emotions that provide pleasurable experience; they delight you and do not impact your body unhealthily. Positive emotions, as expected, promote positive self-development. We are saying that positive emotions are the results of pleasant responses to stimuli in the environment or within ourselves. On the other hand, negative emotions refer to those emotions we do not find particularly pleasant, pleasurable, or delightful to experience. Negative emotions are usually the result of unpleasant responses to stimuli and they cause us to express a negative effect towards a person or a situation.

Naturally, we have different examples of emotions groups under positive and negative. Most times you can't authoritatively state of emotion is positive or negative. There certain emotions could be both positive and negative. The best way to discern between a positive and negative emotion is to use your intuition. For instance, anger could be both, positive and negative. So, the best way to know when it is negative or when it is positive is to intuitively discern the cause and the context of the anger. This book is, of course, going to focus more on negative emotions and how you can embrace them to create positive results for yourself.

Anger and fear are the two prominent negative emotions which most of us erroneously assume we have to do away with. To be realistic, we cannot allow these emotions to rule our lives yet, we must also understand that they are a necessary part of our experiences as humans. It is impossible to say that you never want to get angry anymore; what is possible is to say that you want to control your anger and get angry less. Mastering negative emotions such as anger is about recognizing and embracing the reality of them, determining their source, and becoming aware of their signs so that we can always know when to expect them and how to control them. For example, if you master an emotion like anger, you naturally start to discern which situation may get you angry and how you could avoid this situation.

A list of negative emotions include;

- Anger
- Fear
- Anxiety
- Depression
- Sadness
- Grief
- Regret
- Worry

- Guilt

- Pride

- Envy

- Frustration

- Shame

- Denial...and more.

Many people regard negative emotions to be signs of low emotional intelligence or weakness but this isn't right. Negative emotions have a lot of benefits as long as we do not allow them to overrun us. You aren't completely healthy if you do not let out some negative emotions now and then. One thing you should know is that negative emotions help you consider positive emotions from a counterpoint. If you do not experience negative emotions at all, how then would positive emotions make you feel good? Another thing is that negative emotions are key to our evolution and survival as humans. They direct us to act in ways that are beneficial to our growth, development, and survival as humans. Anger, mostly considered a negative emotion, helps us ascertain and find solutions to problems. Fear teaches us to seek protection from danger; sadness teaches us to find and embrace love and company. It goes on and on like this with every negative emotion there is.

When we talk about negative emotions, we don't mean negative as in "bad." The negativity we talk about certain emotions isn't to portray them as being bad but rather to understand that they lean more towards a negative reality as opposed to positive emotions. Negative emotions, without doubt, can affect our mental and physical state adversely; some primary negative emotions like sadness could result in depression or worry. We must understand that they are designed just for the purpose to make uncomfortable. They could lead to chronic stress when not checked, making us want to escape these emotions. What you should however know is that we cannot completely escape negative emotions; we can only master them so they don't affect us adversely. Often, some of these emotions are geared towards sending us important messages. For example, anxiety may be a telling sign that there is something that needs to be changed and fear may be a sign that a person or situation may endanger the safety.

Overall, what you should know is that these negative emotions you experience aren't something to be gotten rid of. Rather, they are meant to be mastered so we can employ them in achieving the high-functioning, full-of-purpose life that we desire and deserve. Just like positive emotions, negative emotions are meant to protect us and serve as motivation for us to live a better, more qualitative life and build/maintain quality relationships with people around us.

Note: Negative emotions in themselves do not directly have any impact on our mental and physical health and well-being. How we process and react when we experience negative emotions is what matters to our health.

CHAPTER TWO

STRESS

Stress is a major part of our everyday life; it is something we experience now and then. In the medical context, stress defines as a physical, emotional, or mental state of tension in the body. Every day, we have tons of things to get done and we can become stressed when we become overloaded with these demands of our lives. This is what causes stress. Like anxiety, stress is triggered when we have the fight or flight reaction telling us about potential danger and the best way to react to the perceived danger.

Stress is a motivating emotion but it can become challenging to our health and wellbeing when it goes beyond control. Sometimes, stress can even be a trigger for extreme anxiety. Stress may be external, caused by social, environmental, or psychological situations; it can also be internal, caused by an illness or medical procedure.

Usually, the body reacts to major or perceived changes that require adjustments with stress. An example is when you are getting married or moving to a new home. One thing so many people don't know of stress, however, is that it can be both positive and negative, depending on how you react to it. When positive, stress keeps us alert and warns us about impending danger; it serves as a motivator. But when stress becomes negative, it makes a person face challenges continuously without relief from stressors. Due to this, the person may become overly worn out and develops a buildup of bodily tensions.

The fight or flight response is a built-in physiological response activated by the autonomic nervous system when the body has to combat situations that are perceived to be stressful. However, when stressful situations become prolonged, the autonomic nervous system activates this response chronically without stop. This could take an immense emotional and physical toll on the body and mind. When stress continues without stopping, it becomes distressed i.e. a negative reaction to stress. Distress upsets the body's balance and equilibrium thereby resulting in symptoms of stress such as increased blood pressure, headache, discomfort in the chest, and inability to sleep. Distress may also result in emotional problems such as anxiety, depression, and unchecked anger.

According to studies, stress can become extreme and result in worse things than anxiety or depression. It can develop into acute diseases. In fact stress is linked to cancer, heart problems, accidents, cirrhosis of the liver, and other ailments which are some of the leading causes of death. When stress becomes overbearing, it may cause you to turn to the use of substances and other addictions to keep your mind sane. But, what you may not know is that substance abuse and addiction do not relieve stress and return the body to equilibrium. Rather, it keeps your body trapped in a stressed state and worsen the level of stress such that other medical conditions may arise.

Stress comes in three different forms and none of this is helpful to the body in any way. Understanding the kind of stress you are dealing with helps you devise better ways to cope with the stress. According to the American Psychological Association, there are three types of stress which are: acute stress, episodic acute stress, and chronic stress. All forms of stress pose some form of danger to our body but we tend to ignore the worse of them all, chronic stress.

Acute stress is the most common form of stress which all of us have to deal with at one point or the other. It is caused by overbearing demands and pressures of the present and expected future demands. In little doses, acute stress can be pretty exciting and a rush for the body but it becomes exhausting and exhilarating when it gets too much. Thankfully, acute stress is short-term and cannot actually cause any excessive damage on the body as chronic stress would. Most of us recognize acute stress because it is something that happens occasionally. That feeling you get when you just finish an exhausting argument; that is stress. The mind tends to overplay acute stress though. For instance, that argument you had may continue to play in your head long after it has been concluded, making you unable to sleep. As long as you do not let it get out of hand, acute stress should not interfere with your daily life.

Episodic acute stress occurs when you experience acute stress regularly to the point where it places your life in disarray and disorder. People who suffer episodic acute stress tend to be oversensitive, irritable, short-tempered, and tense all the time. Episodic acute stress is a constant state of mini-crises which makes you feel overburdened by life and the many challenges. If you experience constant episodes of acute stress, you are likely to walk around every day brimming with unchecked anger. This kind of stress has similar symptoms with acute stress but its symptoms are often more complex and longer. Often, it ends up causing a tear and wears in our personal and professional relationships with others. Episodic acute stress poses even greater stress when you resort to unhealthy behaviors like drinking, overeating, gambling, etc. to serve as coping strategies. When not effectively managed, episodic acute stress could extend into clinical depression.

Chronic stress is the most serious type of stress and is usually caused by serious life problems which are usually overbearing and beyond control. This kind of stress can wear us down over the years with unrelenting demands which never seem to stop trooping in; they make you feel like you could never have time for other things in your life. You barely manage to get day by day. Chronic stress is long-term and it leaves you with no hope, causing you to surrender yourself wholly to whatever is to come. In some cases of chronic stress, the stress starts from childhood due to certain traumatic experiences and it becomes internalized to the point where it no longer goes away. The most awful thing about chronic stress is that it gets to a point where you no longer remember it is there. It becomes a part of you, a familiar, never-ending, and almost comfortable feeling. However, when chronic stress becomes a part of you like this, it could lead to heart problems, suicide, violence to self, and progress to a complete breakdown of the body system. Chronic stress is especially difficult to treat but the symptoms can be minimized using some of the stress management techniques we will be checking out. With extensive medical care and treatment, you can further manage chronic stress and stop it from adversely affecting your life and relationships.

Some of the symptoms of stress which you should always watch out for are;

- Constant migraine
- Inability to sleep
- Pain and discomfort in the back and neck area
- Dizziness
- Irritability
- Increased heart rate
- Tensed muscles
- Inability to focus
- Depleted energy level
- Turbulence in the mind...and many more.

Difference between Stress and Anxiety

Stress and anxiety share some similar symptoms which make it easy to confuse one for the other. Therefore, it is important to know if you are suffering from stress and anxiety to make healthy coping techniques work. Normal stress is short-term while anxiety is a continual state of mental health which is usually triggered by stress. Even with treatment and healthy coping techniques, anxiety doesn't go away. It is always there, in the shadow. In the next chapter, we will look more extensively at anxiety and the underlying causes.

SOURCES OF STRESS

Stress can originate from different sources; there are several causes of stress. Every day, different types of stressors get triggered and these stressors cause the tension, anxiety, concern, and worry we experience every day. Note that stress can have more than one source so understanding where your stress is originating from can help you learn to cope with the stress, reduce it, and even relieve yourself of it. Even when you go for professional therapy to combat your stress, the therapist has to identify the source of the stress before they can help you with effective stress management techniques to treat the.

As we said, stress can originate from different sources. However, there are 6 most prominent and widely acknowledged sources of stress even by professionals. These are;

- Psychological stress
- Environmental stress
- Physiological stress
- Social stress
- Organizational stress
- Significant events stress

Psychological stress originates from the mind; it is based on your thoughts, perception, and context you create around stressful situations. Your mind is a very powerful tool and it can shape how your body reacts to stressors. Psychological stress occurs when you make irrational conclusions of the feelings and thoughts you have about your stressful situations. It is also referred to as emotional stress or mental stress and is usually induced by strong feelings and emotions.

Environmental stress is one of the main sources of stress and hassle in everybody's daily life. It has to do with stressors in the environment causing you stress. In our environment and surroundings, there are plenty of stressors that increase our stress level every day. An example is living in a noisy street; this can activate stressors and make you exhibit signs of stress and experience the effects of stress.

Physiological stress is another source of stress symptoms and effects. It involves the body's reaction and responses to stressful situations. It is sometimes referred to as physical stress too based on the many physical symptoms of stress you exhibit. The responses your body gives when you are in a stressful situation are what we refer to as a physiological source of stress. An example is a throbbing headache and tensed muscle you experience when you are stressed.

Social stress refers to the stress that originates from the socialization, communication, and interactions we share with other human beings around us. Social stress has to do with the kind of relationship you have with other people. There are some relationships we have which could be highly stressful and tension-filled; they make for very bad experiences. Some may be enjoyable because they produce a positive type of stress which helps us get ahead.

Organizational stress focuses more on the stress that originates from the workplace. Some experts classify this source of stress under environmental stress since it has to do with our work environments majorly; it is stress that comes from work and job. Organizational stress occurs due to the demands and the pressure from the organization, company, or boss you work for. It can be tedious and never-ending.

The final source of stress is the stress of significant events that originate from important, critical, and significant events in life. Usually, this source of stress is positive but there are times when it could be negative too. Some significant events that take place in our life are the source of positive stress; an example is a wedding ceremony or graduation ceremony. However, there are also critical events that trigger negative stress; examples are physical abuse or assault, major accident, loss of someone dear, and other critical events. These kinds of events are often accompanied by a high level of stress which further results in anxiety. They often involve continuing trauma even after the event and this kind of stress are referred to as Post-traumatic stress disorder (PTSD) by experts.

The different sources of stress for humans may be further broken down into causes which are;

- Work

The APA has released data to reveal that work is one of the most common stressors for humans. Work-induced stress can come in different forms such as unemployment, job insecurity, conflict at work, dissatisfaction and overworking. Putting your job ahead of everything else in your life can affect your mental and physical health. This is a form of organizational stress.

- Personal relationships

Sometimes, the stress we experience isn't caused by our work; it is caused by people we share close relationships with. This could be a family member, our partner, close friend, or colleague at work. These people may be toxic to our health without us recognizing it. The stress they cause us can really affect our mental and emotional health. For instance, a romantic relationship sometimes comes with a lot of pressure which could take a toll on your, your partner, and the relationship.

- Financial problems

Money is one of the most common sources of stress among people, if not the most common. According to a study by the American Psychological Association, about 72 percent of people are stressed about money at least sometimes in a month. People are constantly worried about finances and bills and this could release a very high level of stress. Financial insecurity is a common problem and it is only understandable that it will be a stress trigger.

- Parenting

If you are a parent, then your stress level will probably be very high if unchecked. Parents often have to manage a job, raise the kids, and manage their own lives. These demands on them can trigger very high parenting stress. Due to the level of stress, a parent may become overly irritable, harsh, and commanding in handling interactions with the kids. The quality of a parent-child relationship can be negatively affected by parenting stress. If you constantly argue with your kid, it may be due to the irritability caused by parenting stress. Parenting stress may be due to marital problems, low income, working longer hours at work, etc.

- Daily life

Day-to-day stressors are those things that make us want to pull our hair out in frustration. These are things like running late for work or school, misplacing the car key, or losing an important item. Although these are very minor things they could trigger stress and anxiety when they become too frequent, resulting in psychological and physical symptoms. Being busy all the time is another thing that serves stressor and is very common. Nowadays, we have all become very busy with different responsibilities and with this busyness comes a lot of stress.

STRESS MANAGEMENT TECHNIQUES AND TIPS

Stress management has to do with finding out the cause of your stress, whether an internal or external factor and working towards changing them and using them to your advantage. External factors are the challenges you are faced with in your everyday life while internal factors determine how you react and respond to stress induced by these external factors.

The first thing to do before starting stress management is to realize and believe that your life is in your control, not in the control of these internal or external factors. Once you realize this, it becomes easier to manage your stress and keep it in check. Stress management is all about taking charge of your emotions, thoughts, and your perception of any challenge you are facing. This is why mastering your emotions can help keep stress and anxiety at bay.

Stress management begins with identifying and recognizing the source (s) of stress in your life. This may seem to be easy but it is never as easy as it sounds. It is very difficult to identify your source of stress, especially when they are more than one. It is very easy for you to overlook the true cause of your stress. Of course, you would know that there is something that causes you to worry and feel stressed but you may not know what exactly it is. For example, if you are the type who is constantly worried about meeting work deadlines; you may not be able to tell if it is the job itself or procrastination from your side that causes the deadline stress. To recognize the true source (s) of your stress, take an in-depth look at your behaviors, habits, feelings, and thoughts. When you do this, you would be able to tell where exactly the stress is coming from. Recognizing the source of your stress starts with accepting responsibility for the part you play in creating and enabling your stressor; not doing this will forever keep your stress level out of your control.

Do you have a journal where you pen down your everyday feelings, thoughts, and events? If you don't already have one, then it's time you do. Keeping a stress journal helps you recognize the stressors in your everyday life so you can cope with them better. Every time something triggers your stress, make a record of it in your journal. The more you do this, the easier it becomes for you to see common patterns that may otherwise have been hidden. Write down things you know that make you feel stressed, the kind of physical and emotional reactions they trigger, how you react in response to these triggers, and what you do to make yourself feel better. This will make it possible for you to create a stress-coping technique that is personalized to your stressors, triggers, and responses.

Employ the use of stress relievers because these can be effective in coping with stress. There are stress relief techniques that can help calm the body in a matter of minutes; they provide a quick and immediate fix that helps your body become calm at the moment and this can be helpful. Some breathing exercises and meditation techniques are stress relieves you can learn and use whenever your body activates the fight or flight response and trigger stress. There are also relaxation techniques you can learn to control stress and enhance your physical and emotional wellbeing. Although there are meditation techniques that you can only learn in a group or licensed class for effective results, you can also learn some techniques on your own. These are some of the techniques you can use for relief from stress;

- **Biofeedback:** This is one of the widely used methods of relaxation learning which you can use to control stressors and stress responses. In biofeedback, monitoring equipment is used to control stress responses and modify the body's physiological responses using information gotten from the body which would otherwise be unavailable. This method was developed based on the principle that the autonomic nervous system can be trained. The monitoring equipment is used to examine things like heart rate, blood pressure, muscle tension, thinking patterns, etc. Using the feedback gotten from monitoring the body, you can then identify how your stress level is and determine which process works better for achieving your desired result.

- **Autogenic training:** This is a highly effective method of stress management which was developed in the 20th century. It revolves around awareness and concentration on bodily sensations. Using what is known as autogenic formulas, you try to concentrate on various body sensations like warmth or tingling in several parts of your body. Autogenic training is used as part of professional therapy for different conditions, including stress and anxiety. There is no particular skill required in learning this method but you must be willing to invest the amount of time required. The autogenic method of relaxation is however more complex than other methods so you may want to get a course specifically for training.

- **Imagery:** Also referred to as guided imagery, this is a highly efficient 'quick fix' method for managing stress. It focuses on the use of relaxing images to calm the mind and the body. All you need to do is find somewhere quiet, practice breathes control, and envision a pleasant and soothing image in your mind using visualization; this puts you in an immediate state of deep relaxation. Guided imagery is an easy to learn method which you should endeavor to make a daily practice.

- **Meditation:** You can also try out varying meditation techniques to help you cope with stress. Meditation, especially mindfulness, is one of the most widely known techniques for achieving physical and mental calm. Meditation has to do with tuning out of the noise around you and concentrating on the core of the self. It can either be structured or unstructured. At the end of the book, you will be learning some meditation techniques and practices which you can always use.

- **Progressive Muscle Relaxation:** This is a relaxation method that works for stress, anxiety and other conditions which require relaxation. It is a practice in which you tighten your muscle groups and then relax them immediately; you do this over and over till relaxation is achieved. This method was developed based on the idea that mental relaxation naturally results in physical relaxation.

Progressive muscle relaxation requires no special skill except the muscle activity involved. Patience and regular practice are key to achieving the best result with this method. Consistency produces maximum benefits to physical and mental health.

Another method you can use to manage stress is the 4 As of stress management which is an actually popular method which many people use in getting rid of stress. The 4 As of stress management goes as follow;

- Avoid
- Alter
- Adapt
- Accept

The first A is to **avoid stress**, especially when it is unnecessary. One thing about stress is that not all stress is negative therefore you shouldn't avoid all stressful situations. There are some situations that will only get worse, become unhealthy, and turn into anxiety when avoided. Rather than avoid, find out how these situations affect you by making a deep assessment. Doing this makes it possible for you to make a change in situations. The first thing you can do to always avoid unnecessary stress is to start saying "No" to some demands. Sometimes, something may be out of your limit but you still make it an obligation to get this thing done for the person or people involved. Start saying no to certain situations, friends, family, and people who usually make many but it actually isn't. Rather than doing this though, try to talk to someone about the feeling demands of you. Also, avoid and say no to distractions and things that make it impossible for you to focus. Again, ensure you organize and manage all the tasks you have. Doing this is the best way to not miss job deadlines and avoid unnecessary stress.

The second A is to **alter the stressful situation**. There are times when you can't avoid a situation; the best thing to do in times like this is to alter the situation. For instance, when you are faced with stress caused by an upcoming exam, you may want to keep to yourself since you cannot avoid the examination. In this case, keeping all that emotions bottled in may seem like the right thing to do but it isn't. Rather than doing this though, try to talk to someone about the feelings, emotions, and frustrations. Holding everything in could affect your mental and physical health negatively. The only way to alter a stressful situation is to express your feelings and prevent stress from consuming you. You can do this by talking to someone you are close with or keeping a stress journal as we have already said.

The third A says you should **adapt to the stressor**. Most times, there is absolutely nothing you can do to change a stressor. In cases like this, you are the one who needs to change. What you need to do is change your perception of the stressor, the stress, and let your reactions towards the stressor change. Reconstructing your perception of the stressor is one of the ways you can get yourself to adapt to it. Once you start perceiving stressors from a point of view that isn't really negative, your stress becomes easier to manage.

Finally, some situations aren't changeable so in this case, you **accept** these situations. Nothing you do will alter or change some situations so you have to get used to them and accept the reality. For example, there is absolutely nothing you do that will make an examination or test go away, so accept this and make moves to keep the stress they induce under control. Create a helpful schedule that you can follow to makes stress as minimal as possible and keep it at bay.

Whenever you have to deal with a stressful situation, remind yourself of the 4 As and put them to use with other stress management techniques we have checked out!

CHAPTER THREE

ANXIETY

Anxiety is one of the common secondary emotions; it is usually experienced in the place of another emotion which a person cannot adequately feel or even express. Anxiety may be a secondary emotion to anger. In itself, anxiety is a normal and sometimes healthy emotion which we experience when we are faced with what we consider a difficult or challenging situation. It is also a natural response to stress; it is usually triggered as a result of fear or apprehension. But, anxiety can become a medical disorder when it becomes overwhelming and starts interfering with our daily activities. When feelings of anxiety become extreme and last well beyond six months, they become an anxiety disorder.

Anxiety disorders are usually categorized by excessive worry, fear, and nervousness. Anxiety could alter how you process your emotions and behave in reaction to these emotions. Anxiety may be mild or extreme. Mild anxiety is the type that leaves you feeling slightly unsettled while extreme cases of anxiety usually have a large adverse effect on your day-to-day living.

According to the American Psychological Association (APA), anxiety may be defined as "an emotion characterized by feelings of tensions, worried thoughts, and physical changes such as increased blood pressure." As a healthy and functioning human being, it is normal to experience occasional feelings of anxiety. However, it becomes extreme and severe when our level of anxiety becomes highly disproportionate.

There is a difference between normal anxiety and anxiety disorders. As humans, anxiety is a normal emotion we experience when we face potentially harmful situations because it is necessary for our evolution and survival. When humans face potential danger, certain bodily alarms are set off in the body to alert us and trigger an evasive reaction. These alarms come in the form of increased heartbeat, sweating, trembling, and heightened sensitivity to the surroundings. The cause of this is the trigger of a hormone called adrenaline. When we sense danger, our body releases a rush of adrenaline which activates certain anxious responses in what has been termed the "fight-or-flight" response. The fight-or-flight response makes us run from a dangerous situation. While the fight-or-flight response was engineered back when humans were still quite primitive, it has evolved into more contemporary things.

Feelings of anxiety are now being triggered by work, family, lifestyle, money, and other crucial things that command our attention and sets off adrenaline without actually requiring the fight-or-flight response. Those nervous feelings we get in a difficult situation or right before an important event mirrors the original fight-or-flight reaction. For example, when you get anxious about walking the streets at night, you will instinctively try to avoid possible danger if you do walk the street at night.

Ordinary anxiety serves as motivation to us and increases our chances of survival in our environment but anxiety moves beyond normal to a medical disorder when it becomes unnecessarily delayed or extremely severe or when it goes out of proportion to the anxiety trigger. Anxiety may manifest in the form of physical symptoms such as increased blood level, nausea, and so on, and all of these could be damaging to our wellbeing.

CAUSES OF ANXIETY

Over the years, there has been much research conducted to identify the underlying cause of anxiety but the cause of anxiety remains largely unknown. But, certain factors could serve as triggers for anxiety. Anxiety may occur as a result of the combination of two or more of these factors. Certain events, emotions, and experiences may also serve as triggers for feelings of anxiety or complicate them. People have individual anxiety triggers but some are triggers that are common among the majority of the anxious population. Some people experience anxiety attacks without any trigger at all. To control your anxiety, you must identify what serves as a trigger for it. Identifying the factors and triggers that encourage feelings of anxiety in you is key to managing anxiety. In truth, you cannot actually manage anxiety but you can manage the triggers so that anxiety becomes reduced or mild.

According to research, anxiety may be a genetic inheritance. Having a close family member with anxiety problems increases an individual's chances of experiencing anxiety issues. However, there has been no solid or substantial proof to discern whether anxiety inherited genetically is the result of certain genetic factors or the result of learning and adapting from our parents or primary caretakers. A difficult childhood experience may serve as a trigger for anxiety; this is even one of the most common triggers identified by experts. If you had a traumatic and highly stressful childhood growing up, there is the likelihood that you will develop huge anxiety problems as an adult. Emotional abuse, neglect, grief, physical abuse, social isolation, and bullying are some of the childhood experiences which can become triggers for anxiety. For instance, a person who was raised by emotionally inconsistent parents is likely to develop problems of anxiety. Separation anxiety is something that occurs when a child is separated from a primary caregiver from a very young age; it could be mild or acute, causing huge emotional trauma for the child.

Anxiety problems may also be triggered by certain health issues. When health issues serve as triggers for anxiety the result is usually very powerful due to the immediate feelings it stimulates. One of the health issues which could be a trigger for anxiety is any problem related to the heat. In fact, experts say that individuals with generalized anxiety disorder are more prone to heart attacks and other heart diseases than other people. A chronic health issue such as cancer could be the trigger for your anxiety. Living with a life-threatening health condition can be really disheartening, especially if it is one that has gone beyond a cure. It puts you in a constant state of fear, distress, worry, and apprehension about what is to come or what the future holds; this serves as a trigger for anxiety or anxiety attacks. Diabetes, hyperthyroidism, asthma, chronic obtrusive pulmonary disease, and chronic pains are some of the other health problems which could trigger symptoms of anxiety. The best way to tackle anxiety caused by health issues is to become proactive and very aware of your situation. You may also reach out to a therapist to help manage the emotions being evoked by the results of your diagnosis.

Certain medications and over-the-counter prescriptions can also trigger feelings of anxiety. Sometimes, anxiety arises as a side-effect to the use of these medications. This because some ingredients in these medications give you feelings of unease or being unwell; they make you queasy. When you have these unsettling feelings of unease, another series of events may be triggered in your mind or body, resulting in more symptoms of anxiety. Medications such as cough medications, weight loss pills, and birth control pills trigger symptoms of anxiety. Recreational and psychiatric medications may also trigger anxiety problems. If you do not have close relatives with anxiety or never experienced trauma or emotional/physical abuse as a child, then the cause of your anxiety may be a certain medication you are taking.

You probably love caffeine so much but do you even know it could be the source of your anxiety problem? Many of us like to start our day with a cup of pleasant coffee; it can be refreshing. However, a study conducted in 2010 has revealed that caffeine has some anxiety-inducing effects in which people with panic disorder (a form of anxiety disorder) are especially susceptible to. Caffeine is a stimulant; it has the same effect on your mind and body that a frightening situation would. When you consume caffeine, it stimulates the fight or flight response which could heighten your anxiety and trigger an anxiety attack. Too many cups of caffeine will leave you feeling moody, jittery, nervous, and sleepless and all of these could definitely worsen your anxiety symptoms. Some foods and drinks can also trigger or worsen symptoms of anxiety. An example is a sugar and alcoholic drinks.

You probably didn't know this but cutting back on food consumption could trigger anxiety problems. When you skip meals, your blood sugar level drops and this results in a rumbling tummy and jittery and sweaty hands. You have to eat balanced meals appropriately. Eating gives you much-needed energy and nutrients with which you keep your body and mind healthy and functioning. If you are the type who is too busy to eat three times a day as you should, then ensure you have a variety of healthy snacks at hand to make up for the lost meals. This will help prevent low blood sugar, nervousness, and anxiety symptoms. Also, keep it in mind that certain foods may affect your mood positively or negatively.

Just like the pioneer of cognitive theories of emotions suggested, our thoughts have a large and unwavering impact on our emotional and physical state. The mind is the anchor of the body and this reflects with people who have anxiety problems. For instance, your choice of thoughts or words when you are scared, frustrated, or angry may trigger feelings of anxiety even when you don't expect it. If you are the type who employs the use of negative words and thinking in your perception of yourself, it can largely trigger some primary emotions which aggravate anxiety. For instance, if you have a very important test coming up and your first choice of words to yourself is "Oh, there's no way I'll pass this test," your mind accepts this as an affirmation that you cannot pass the test. Then, feelings of stress, worry, and helplessness set in to further increase your physiological anxiety reactions.

Some risk factors increase a person's chance of developing anxiety symptoms. Apart from trauma, grief, or abuse, some other risk factors which could trigger symptoms of anxiety are stress, stress buildup, personality disorders, etc. For instance, some problems in your life and seemingly difficult situations may result in the buildup of stress which in turn causes anxiety symptoms to be triggered. Some of these problems include financial problems, overworking, unemployment, undue pressure, etc. There are also other stressors that we continually experience in our daily life.

Anger as a trigger for Anxiety

Like we said, anxiety is usually experienced as a secondary emotion. So, which major primary emotion could be a trigger for anxiety? The answer is anger! Yes, you and very self-critical; chronic worriers don't seem like the type to get an didn't expect that answer since most people who have anxiety problems tend to be kind, polite, and very self-critical; chronic worriers obviously don't seem like the type to get angry. Well, the keyword here is "obviously" which explains how we all seem to miss the fact that anger could be a trigger for anxiety.

Often, anxiety is associated with fear and fear is regarded as the polar opposite of anger. What you may not know however is that fear is sometimes a trigger of anger which may further become a source of anxiety. Some people get angry because they feel weak expressing feelings of worries or concerns so they resort to covering this up with anger. For others, anger is a core symptom of underlying anxiety problems and anger-anxiety is usually linked to the fight or flight reaction that occurs when we face a difficult situation. Some people experience severe anxiety due to episodic anger, the fear of losing control, and the stress that comes with having to bottle anger in.

Firstly, anger is a very strong emotion that can induce great health consequences. How does anger even trigger anxiety? Anger serves as a trigger to anxiety when it is bottled in rather than being let out through a healthy avenue. This problem starts from as early as childhood and is encouraged by society. From a young age, we are taught that anger is a bad thing; it is rude, impolite, and should never be expressed because it makes us go out of control. This, of course, results in anger denial as adults. Due to the many beliefs, we have been fed about anger as kids, we tend to repress this emotion rather than express it. However, when you deny or repress a feeling, this feeling doesn't necessarily go away; instead, it is channeled towards another place. Acting like you are unoffended when someone upsets you doesn't make your anger go away, it is akin to setting off a time bomb. The fact that we are made to believe that feelings that give us no pleasure are not meant to be acknowledged or expressed can cause even bigger problems such as feelings of shame, low self-esteem, and confusion. In time, we may learn to accept the cause of our anger as being normal instead of refuting or fighting against it. For instance, if as a child, you were bullied by an older person but you have been taught never to express your anger; your mind becomes conditioned to bottle anger in rather than express it.

When the fight or flight response is activated without any seeming danger or risk, it could result in a series of complex anger-related emotions which further heighten the level of anxiety. These include;

- **Irritation**: Anxiety as an emotion makes a person susceptible to annoyance and irritation which happens to be some of the foremost negative triggers of anger. People who are constantly irritated usually feel bothered by the company and they tend to react with anger. They may also become upset by their anxiety in general and choose to make anger an outlet for their frustration.

- **Loss of control**: Sometimes, anger is a person's natural response to situations where they feel like they aren't in control. Anxiety may make a person feel as though they have no form of control over some situations; this is quite common among people who experience anxiety attacks

Conclusively, as much as we understand that anger may be a symptom of anxiety, we must also recognize the fact that it could also be a major cause or trigger for anxiety. People with anger problems tend to especially feel high levels of stress which further leads to more stress and anxiety. Sometimes, when not effectively checked, anger and anxiety can become a cycle you become trapped in.

So, how can you control your anxiety by mastering emotions such as anger and fear which are the primary emotional triggers? Let's find out!

CURBING ANXIETY BY MASTERING YOUR EMOTIONS

When you are emotionally intelligent and self-aware of your emotions, it becomes much easier to manage anxiety, especially one triggered by a primary emotion. Your anxiety is in the mind so the best way to manage it is to work the mind against it. The hold anxiety has on your mind can be loosened if you learn to free your mind of all worries and stress while making sure you live totally in the present and not an uncertain future.

Since anxiety happens when the body triggers the fight or flight response without any actual threat due to the surge of stressors in the body, the best way to manage anxiety is to condition your mind to stop seeing a dangerous situation where there is none. Once you do this, your body stops activating the fight or flight reaction without any actual danger.

If you deal with anxiety attacks regularly, then your mind is a very strong one. Therefore, you can harness the strength of your mind fueled by anxiety in fighting against this anxiety itself. The stronger your mind is in the experience of anxiety, the likelier the possibility of turning it against the anxiety so as to manage it. When you do this, anxiety becomes something you are able to control when it comes to visiting rather than an intrusive and obsessive visitor that doesn't allow you to get on with your normal life.

A mindset change is the first step to take in the bid to manage anxiety. Changing your mindset is however not something you can do at once; you need to make it gradual, using small repeated steps. Anxiety is a learned response so it may take quite a while to get the mind to unlearn it. Since anxiety and anxious feelings/thoughts are actually meant to promote our survival and safety, you may find it challenging training your mind to let go of its tight hold on anxiety. We will be giving some strategies to help you curb anxiety better using your anxious mind but, ensure you do not try to use all of the strategies at once. If you try to make everything work at once, your mind may end up giving up in frustration and you would have achieved nothing. Rather, take each of the strategies you will be learning one at a time and do it until your mind becomes accustomed to the process. Remember that when new things seem too challenging, it is always quite easy to go back to what is familiar.

Live in the Present

How does anxiety work? It takes your mind away from the present to an uncertain and unsettling state of "what-ifs and maybes." No matter how strong and calm you feel your mind is, anxiety can do this to you. So, what you should do is train your mind to stay in the future and stop wavering into the future; live in the present and stop worrying about what's to come. For instance, if you have a big test coming up, you'd naturally feel some form of anxiety; however, dwelling in what may happen when you do take the test may only compound your anxiety so rather than worry about the test that is to come, spend that time making active efforts in the present to ensure the test goes as smoothly as possible. Always position your mind in what is happening rather than what may happen. Open all your senses up to your current environment and try to savor the present reality. What can you feel, see, hear, or taste? Concentrate on this; do not live in your mind. When you first start doing this, you may find it quite uncomfortable so try to use a time limit. For instance, you can start by doing this for 2 minutes every day. Each time you do this, your mind becomes stronger at pulling back from feelings of anxiety. As you progress and get better at it, extend the period of time you use. The better you get at it, the longer you should make the time limit. Ensure you make this practice a regular one and develop it into a habit. The more you do it, the stronger your mind gets at pushing away anxiety thoughts and feelings. The brain is an organ that strengthens with experience and this one is an experience that will change your life for the better. For instance: if you constantly get anxious about dying due to a chronic illness or something, try making your mind dwell on something like "I am alive right now. I can feel the breeze against my skin; it feels really cool. I hear the winds rustling and nature smiling. I am safe right now."

Use the Relaxation Response

That message that triggers the fight or flight response and puts you in an anxious state of mind comes from the amygdala, the part of the brain responsible for activating the fight or flight reaction. So, another way to control anxiety is to convince the amygdala that there is nothing to worry about so as to get it to stop being overzealous about its job. However, since you can't just talk to your amygdala and get it to stop, replacing the fight or flight with a relaxation response is something psychologists believe can really help you curb your feelings of anxiety. You need to convince your brain that it has no reason to fight or flee, using your mind.

The relaxation response is a creature of nature that was discovered by Dr. Herbert Benson, a Harvard cardiologist. One good thing about the relaxation response is that it's wired deep in the brain just like the fight or flight response. So, you don't have to worry if it could even work; it will definitely work once you learn to activate it. It is automatic so it can be activated whether you need it or not. When the relaxation response is triggered, certain neurochemicals are sent out to the brain to immediately halt the fight or flight response. Using the relaxation response can be really helpful because it helps lower heart rate, decrease blood pressure, and lower pulse rate, all of which are the opposite of what happens when you are in an anxious state.

Since the relaxation response is a physiological response, there are many ways you can trigger the reaction. You can try different methods to see which one works best for you. Keep it in mind that the fight or flight response has been in practice for quite a while without interruption so getting your brain to activate a relaxation response when it is in action will take regular practice. With constant practice, you will become good at it and will no longer have to live a life of fear. Start by controlling your breathing. All right, this may sound like something cliché but be patient because it actually works. When you get your breathing under control, you get to reverse all the symptoms associated with an anxious mind like shallow breathing, increased heart rate, etc. When you want to do this, ensure you are sitting quietly in a place without any form of noise; be aware of your breathing and concentrate on it so your mind doesn't drift off, and do not breathe too fast. Slow down your breathing and ensure that you take short pauses between breathing in and out.

Exercise Regularly

Engage in some physical activity. Exercise is so cool; it works for almost anything. When you exercise or engage in other physical activity, your brain tunes out the fight or flight response by getting rid of excess adrenaline and stress hormones so your body can go back to being calm. Since the fight or flight response is usually triggered in order for us to engage in a physical activity that protects us from danger, like fighting or fleeing; exercise may be a great way to convince the brain that it is time to conclude the response because physical activity has already taken place. Try running, sit-ups or fast walks. Here is something to take away: several studies have confirmed that exercising five times a week can make a person less stressed, anxious, or depressed. Everybody knows exercise has an immense benefit for our mental health so don't be afraid to get sweaty.

Know your Symptoms and create Contexts

Some people who struggle with anxiety attacks sometimes confuse it for a heart attack and this makes the symptoms of anxiety get even worse. Whenever you have an anxiety episode, know that it isn't a heart attack. Shortness of breath, pain in the chest, and discomfort in the upper body are just some of the signs of a heart attack which you do not experience during an anxiety or panic attack. Convince your mind that you aren't going nuts; being able to do this is a top sign that you aren't because people who are preoccupied with uncertainty usually don't have the time to worry about the state of their mental health.

One of the reasons why anxiety is so dreadful is because it comes with a lot of anxiety and gives physical feelings and symptoms that seem to portray something much bigger. What you should do is to give context to these feelings and thoughts when they come because simply leaving them to float around as they like may even worsen the duration or severity of the anxiety. When you leave the thoughts alone, your mind may try to convince you that the physical symptoms are pointers to something ominous and you may also feel that the feelings you are having are signs that something bad is about to happen to you. This may become a state of worrying about the worry; a complex form of anxiety.

So, practice creating a context around the anxious feelings and thoughts you have. This may be difficult at first but the more you practice, the stronger you become at calming your mind and stop dwelling on the message you think they contain. Remember that anxiety is a warning to keep you safe from possible danger so envelope yourself with that sense of security and safety. For instance: say something like "I feel my heart racing in my chest and my hands shaking. This is just anxiety; it isn't a sign of a more serious issue. It will soon pass and I will be okay."

Engage your Thoughts and Feelings with Patience

It is easy to get consumed with changing your mindset and get rid of anxious thoughts and feelings to the point where it doesn't work. Thoughts come and go, and so does feelings. Therefore, patience is key to a mindset change. Be patient to know whatever it is you are thinking or feeling. The way anxiety works, it draws you in and keeps you concentrated on every anxious thought or feeling and this could be quite exhausting. Try experimenting with being an observer of your thoughts and feelings, knowing that they will go just as they came. However, do not be in a hurry to get rid of them by pushing them away. There are times when you need to engage with your anxious thoughts and feelings and there are times when you simply sit back and wait for them to dissipate.

Lastly, do not fight against your anxiety. Like we have said, negative emotions aren't something to be fought or gotten rid of, they are meant to be embraced and put under control so this is exactly what you should do with your anxiety. One thing to know about anxiety is that it feeds off of itself so the more you struggle with anxiety, the more anxious you become; you would even become anxious about being anxious. Remember that your mind thinks the anxiety is protecting you and it would never leave until it has done its job. So, accept your anxiety and always remind yourself that it's not more than anxiety. Never forget that anxiety is simply a physical, neurological response of your overzealous and over-vigilant amygdala. Remind yourself of this every time you to activate the relaxation response or other techniques that help put your anxiety under control.

CHAPTER FOUR

ANGER

Anger is often perceived from the point of a primary emotion but anger may also be a secondary emotion. Anger is often more secondary than primary. Anger is a basic human emotion that is connected with our survival as humans. It is as basic as happiness, sadness, fear, and other elemental emotions. Like stress and anxiety, anger is also connected with the "fight or flight" response of the nervous system; it is meant for your protection and survival. The fight or flight response is usually activated when someone perceives danger; it prepares you to either fight or flees from the perceived danger. However, fighting in this response has evolved from actual fighting to other things. There are situations where "fighting" doesn't mean getting your punch ready; it may be reacting to injustice by championing a cause for justice.

Contrary to what you have been made to believe, anger is a perfectly normal, usually healthy, and natural human emotion. But, anger can also become destructive when it gets out of control. We all feel anger at some point in time although in varying degrees. This is because anger is a part of our experiences as humans. Anger usually arises in varying contexts and is usually preceded by some emotion which could be pain, injustice, dissatisfaction, criticism, and unfairness generally. Usually, anger comes in different range from irritation to rage. Anger in the form of mild irritation may be caused by feelings of stress, tiredness, and anxiety. In fact, humans are likely to become irritated when their basic human needs like food, shelter, and sleep are not being met. We may also be irritated by thoughts and opinions from other people who do not conform to ours.

Often, when anger becomes an emotion we cannot control, it becomes destructive. It can have a massive impact on our personal and work relationships with others but it doesn't stop at this. Anger is also destructive to our health, physically and emotionally. With unchecked anger usually comes stress and when anger becomes prolonged, the stress hormones that come with anger can destroy certain neurons in some part of the brain responsible for short-term memory and judgment. Anger can also weaken the immune system.

As we have said, anger is a basic human emotion necessary for survival so there are times when anger can be positive and not "bad." Anger is not a "bad" emotion in itself; it becomes bad when we allow it get to us unchecked i.e. when it becomes uncontrollable. No emotion is necessarily bad as long as we can master and control these emotions. Anger may sometime be a substitute emotion that is being used to cover up for something like pain, envy, jealousy, etc. Some people make themselves angry just so they don't have to feel pain. People change their emotions from pain to anger sometimes because it is easier to be angry than it is to be in pain. This may be a conscious or unconscious action.

Anger is usually grouped into several types by experts and for this book, we will be checking out 8 identified types of anger. Knowing the type or source of your anger makes it easier for this anger to be controlled or managed. All types of anger which we will be examining are psychologically based since anger is an emotion of the mind.

- **Righteous Anger:** This is positive anger that we feel when an injustice has been committed or when we feel a rule has been broken. It may also be referred to as judgmental or moral anger because morally indignant anger may also arise due to our perception of someone else's shortcomings. This kind of anger usually stems from belief and rules. That anger you experience when you feel that someone's human right has been abused is righteous. However, this sort of anger may assume a morally superior stance which is that you think you are better than some people and that is why you get angry with them; it may also be because you think someone is better than something they have done. Righteous anger may become excessive out of the need to manipulate and control others.

- **Assertive Anger:** Have you ever used your feelings of rage to initiate a social good or positive change? If yes, then this is what we refer to as assertive anger. It is a constructive kind of anger that serves a catalyst for initiating changes aimed at positively altering the state of something. Rather than express anger in form of confrontations, arguments, outbursts, and verbal abuse, people who get assertively angry express their rage in ways that create a positive change around the situation that got them angry in the first place. This is normally done without any form of destruction, distress, or anxiety. Assertive anger can be a really powerful motivator for you.

- **Aggressive Anger:** Also called behavioral anger, this type of anger is usually physically expressed. It is a highly volatile, unpredictable, and out-of-control that may push you to physically attack someone. But, this doesn't mean that this anger always results in harm or injuries. When this anger overwhelms you, it may push you to lash out at the object of your anger or something else nearby like the wall or a photo frame. Aggressive or behavioral anger may have huge legal and personal consequences. Trauma or neglect from childhood may be the root of this type of anger.

- **Habitual anger:** There are times when anger becomes a perpetual emotion because you have spent so much time being angry. Habitual anger refers to when you are in a constant state of irritation, dissatisfaction, and unrest such that pretty much everything annoys you. People who have this kind of habitual anger may even get angrier when confronted about their anger or certain situations. The underlying secret behind this kind of anger is that it is always rooted deep in the past and it accumulates over the years probably due to negative experiences. The older you get without managing this anger, the more you feed it.

- **Chronic Anger:** This is a general and dangerous form of anger. It is the absolute and continual resentment of your situation, certain circumstances, people around you and even yourself. It is a form of habitual anger because it is also in perpetuity. Since it is a prolonged experience, chronic anger often has immensely adverse effects on an individual's mental and physical wellbeing.

- **Passive-Aggressive Anger:** People who try to avoid confrontations and expressions of feelings are the ones who usually experience the passive-aggressive type of anger. Passive-aggressive anger has to do with repressing your anger, rage, or fury to avoid getting into arguments and confrontations. This kind of anger is often expressed subtly in the form of sarcasm, verbal abuse, mockery, veiled silence, and chronic procrastination. Most people who express anger passively often don't accept that they are aggressive but their actions may have damaging effects on their personal and professional relationships with others.

- **Verbal Anger:** Often, verbal anger is considered to be milder than aggressive or habitual anger but it is just as bad. This anger is deeply emotional and psychological which has profound effects on the target of the abuse. It comes in the form of threats, mockery, sarcasm, yelling, screaming, furious shouting, blaming, and poor criticism. It is often experienced out of annoyance or irritation.

- **Self-harm:** This is a kind of anger directed by oneself at oneself. It goes way beyond depression. For instance, there some people cut themselves up; this could be them expressing anger because they probably don't like their looks. Self-harm is quite complicated however you should know that it is a very negative emotion which you can't hold in. Self-harm can be a result of so many things;

physical abuse, emotional abuse, neglect, and trauma. It may also be because of repeated disappointments. Rather than expressing their anger towards the person who has wronged them, some people focus the anger on their inner self.

No matter the type of anger you experience, there are some factors that are the major causes of anger. For effective anger management to take place, you must know and address the cause of your anger. So, let's check out some of the known causes of anger.

Factors that Contribute to Anger

Many factors contribute to why you get angry apart from the fact that anger is a natural emotion which you must experience. How you react to situations depend on certain factors in life and these factors are the ones that determine the degree of anger you experienced.

The first known factor that contributes to how you experience anger is your childhood and upbringing. As children, many people have been taught certain beliefs about anger; they were taught that anger is destructive, bad, and very negative. Individuals who were taught that it is bad to express anger learn not to complain about injustice; they may have also been punished for expressing their anger as kids. So, they learn to keep the anger in till it becomes a long-term habitual problem. Sometimes, they end up expressing their anger in very unhealthy ways due to years of bottling all these emotions in. They may also turn the anger inwards if there are no other outlets. Some people have grown up thinking it is okay to be aggressive or violent so they tend to act out their anger aggressively. This may be because they weren't taught how to properly express their emotions or manage them.

Another factor that contributes to anger and how you react to situations is the past experiences you have had. As a child, if you have experienced situations that made you feel angry and resentful in the past but you weren't able to healthily express this anger at the time, you may still be nursing the anger till the present time. For instance, if you have been abused or you have faced trauma in the past, the anger may still be there lurking somewhere in your heart especially if you weren't able to do anything about it then. Of course, this results in you finding some situations particularly difficult and easy to get you angry.

Your anger problem may also be due to circumstances you are presently faced with and not just things you experienced in the past. Current circumstances and challenges may leave you feeling angrier than normal or make you get angry at things and situations that aren't even related. If there is a situation making you angry and you can't do anything about it, you may express the anger at other times under a totally different condition. As an example, if your boss at work makes you angry and stressed out every day but you can't do anything about it since he's your boss, you may express the anger at home rather than at work. For instance, you may get home and lash at the kids or your spouse grumpily or angrily and then blame it on a "long day."

These are 3 of the most influencing factors for what gets you angry and how you react to potentially raging situations.

Anger as a Positive Emotion

As much as we all like to consider anger a negative emotion, it can also be a positive emotion when we react to it the right way; it is also positive as long as we have our anger under control and never let it consume us. When anger is positive, it means it is driving us to do something beneficial; positive anger lays the foundation for changes and developments.

Positive anger is a highly motivating force that compels us to do something we may have thought we couldn't do in the past. Anger fuels our passion and drives us towards our goals no matter the challenges and barriers that seem to be in our way. It is a constructive kind of emotion that infuses us with the energy and motivation needed to get what we want; it can inspire a clamor for social change and justice (think Martin Luther King). Again, when anger is a positive emotion, it pushes us to be optimistic. Now, this may sound odd and impossible to you but it is true. Anger could make you optimistic just like happiness does.

Anger as a positive emotion can also be very beneficial to our relationships. It is a natural emotion and we have to strive to be as natural as possible in our relationships. There is no need to suck it in and repress your anger with a smile when your partner, relative, or friend wrongs you. According to research, anger becomes negative and detrimental to a relationship when you suppress or hide it. When you repress your anger and give a faux smile, you are not letting your partner know what they have done to wrong you so they may keep doing it which doesn't do the relationship good. However, when you express your anger positively and healthily, it strengthens your relationship and the bond you share with your partner. Anger helps you find solutions to whatever problem you have in your relationships.

Anger can also be positive when we use it for self-insight; this emotion is a pretty good tool for examining and looking inwards ourselves. Anger allows us to see our faults and work on them. If you never express your anger, there is every chance that you would never know what you doing wrong to people to get that reaction which triggers your anger. Sometimes, the fault is with you and not the person who made you angry. When you become self-conscious and self-aware, you can find ways through which you can channel your anger to improve your life for the better. Positive anger promotes positive self-change.

Okay, this next one sounds absolutely odd but what if you learned that anger reduces violence? Yes, it absolutely does. We all know that anger is an emotion that is known to precede violence so how can anger even reduce violence? What happens is that when you get angry, it may be a powerful pointer telling you that something needs to be changed or resolved. When you notice this, anger could motivate you to take actions to mediate the situation which could instigate violence if not checked. Take a moment and imagine a world where no one could react to injustice immediately with anger? Yeah, it does seem like a potentially violent world. Also, when someone wrongs us and we express our anger healthily, it may make them take actions to placate us and right the wrong they committed.

Finally, positive anger can be used to get what you want. One thing you should keep in mind at all time though is that anger can only be positively or used positively when it is justifiable. Anger which makes you feel control is not positive and cannot be used to initiate positive developments or changes. This is the kind of anger you'll need the anger management techniques we will be discussing for. Anger management techniques teach you to transform your anger from positive to negative.

DESTRUCTIVE EFFECTS OF HAVING AN ANGER PROBLEM

Have you ever heard of the saying "A thought murder a day keeps the doctor away?" This saying is a quite insightful one which refers to how letting yourself feel angry is a healthy thing to do whereas suppressing or denying feelings of anger can have an immensely pathological effect on you. From past experiences, what we have come to know about anger is that it only becomes destructive to you or people around you when it is repressed or let out unhealthily. Anger can have profoundly negative effects on you, your happiness, and the people around you. Suppressing your feelings of anger has utterly destructive consequences. When you repress your anger, you have the tendency of becoming psychosomatic which could cause real harm to your body. Holding in your anger creates tension in the body and this may cause stress which is a major player in many of the psychosomatic illnesses which we have. Based on research done in the past, there have been substantial evidence to prove that suppressing anger can be the precursor to cancer development in the body and may also inhibit progress even after the cancer has been diagnosed and is being treated.

There are so many effects anger could have on your health. Let's examine some of these effects.

- **Heart Problems:** Anger puts you at great risk of having a heart attack. The risk of having a heart attack doubles whenever you have an outburst of anger. When you suppress your anger or express it through an unhealthy outlet, the effect goes directly to your heart meaning it could lead to heart problems. In fact, a study has shown that people with anger disorders or volatile anger are more likely to have coronary disease more than people who show less signs of anger. However, constructive or positive anger is in no way related to any heart problem. It could even be very good for your health.

- **Weak Immune System:** Getting angry all the time can actually weaken the immune system, making you prone to more and more illnesses as a study has confirmed. Based on a study conducted in Harvard Medical School, an angry outburst can cause a 6-hour drop in the amount of immunoglobulin A, an antibody responsible for defending the body against infections. Now, imagine if you are always angry; you could really damage your immune system unless you learn to control your anger.

- **Cause Stroke:** You are at a very high risk of having a severe stroke if you are the type who explodes every time. Volatile and habitual anger increases your possibility of developing a stroke ranging from a slightly mild blood clot to the brain to actual bleeding in the brain.

- **Increase Anxiety:** Experiencing anxiety at one point or the other is a normal thing but anger can actually worsen your anxiety if care is not taken. In fact, anger is a primary emotion to anxiety i.e. your anxious feelings may be due to underlying anger problems. Anger increases the symptoms of Generalized Anxiety Disorder (GAD) which is an extreme case of anxiety. People with GAD have higher levels of repressed, internalized, and unexpressed anger which contributes to the development of GAD symptoms; this can be quite destructive.

- **Causes Depression:** Anger increases anxiety which can ,in turn, result in clinical depression. Over the years, many studies have found a link between anger, anxiety, and depression, especially when it comes to men. Passive anger is one of the symptoms of depression; you are constantly angry but too unmotivated to act on the anger.

- **Decreases Lifespan:** Anger results in stress and stress is a very strong suspect when it comes to ill health. Combined with stress, anger can have a really strong effect on your health and it can shorten your lifespan due to the number of health problems it can generate. People who constantly experience repressed anger have shorter lifespans than people who express their anger healthily.

Anger should never be repressed or unhealthily expressed. Instead, you should take active efforts to manage your anger and put it under control so as to avoid all of the negative effects of anger which you have just learned about. Never should you try to stifle or suppress your anger. Suppressing emotions as we have reiterated over the chapters makes it hard to manage them or master them like you should. To start with, pay attention to any feeling of anger you experience and use the information gained to discern where the anger is coming from so that you can use one or more of the anger management techniques we will be checking out below to effectively combat anger problems.

MASTERING YOUR EMOTIONS TO MANAGE ANGER EFFECTIVELY

Generally, people consider anger management to be about anger suppression or repression. But, it is not about that at all. It is not a healthy choice to never express your anger. In fact, anger is a healthy emotion which you should always express when necessary or justified. No matter how hard you try to suppress anger, you will always show the signs. And, anger only becomes volatile when you have held it in for so long.

The goal of anger management is to help you understand where your anger is coming from and the underlying emotion behind it so that you can find ways to express it without losing your cool. When you know the place your anger is coming from, you not only find it easier to express this anger healthily, it also strengthens you so that you can manage your life and relationships better.

Mastering your emotions to achieve anger management requires a lot of patience, diligence, and practice which means you must be willing and ready to put the hard work in. Once you achieve your anger management goals, the results can be pretty rewarding and fulfilling. With anger management, you can build and develop better relationships, improve your mental and physical health, chase you dreams, achieve you goals, and ultimately improve the quality of life you lead.

The first step in anger management is **identifying the cause or**

trigger of your anger. What makes you angry? Is your anger a standalone emotion or is it a substitute for another emotion? Or, maybe it is even a secondary emotion which stems from another related emotion? Ask yourself: "what am I really angry about?" Look deep within yourself and your situation to identify the real source of your anger. If you have ever gotten into a big fight over something really little, it must have left you feeling really silly and you must have wondered what was wrong with you at a point. So, take time out to search within yourself and try to identify that cause. Is it some other feeling like shame, fear, or insecurity? Are you so angry because of some trauma from childhood or were you subdued as a child? Maybe your anger is even a learned behavior? In some cases, your anger may also be due to situations out of your control or certain people in your life. However, this doesn't mean you should pin the blame of your anger on other people. It is more to do with learning the exact source or trigger so you can work on it, whether it is a person, experience or current situation. Once you learn the source of your anger, it becomes very easy to move on to the next step of anger management which is to recognize your anger warning signs.

How do you tell when you are about to experience a sudden anger outburst? You **become self-aware of the preceding signs** before you lose control and get all angry. Many people feel that anger is an immediate emotion like you can just explode into anger without a forewarning but it doesn't work like that. Before a violent angry outburst, your body gives you some physical warning signs that you need to start looking out for. Becoming self-aware and recognizing the different signs your body gives before explosive anger is crucial to anger management because then, you can learn to tame your anger before it goes out of your control. Some of the telling signs you may have right before an anger episode are;

- Faster breaths
- Knots in the stomach
- A flushed feeling
- Tightly clenched jaw or fists
- Pounding heart
- Tensed muscles and shoulders
- Lack of concentration
- A detachment from logic and understanding

Once you recognize your anger telling signs, the next step to take is to **determine if the bridling anger is a friend or your enemy**. There are fit of anger you need to express and those you need to tame and put under control. You should always express any anger that seems like a friend and keep the one that seems like an enemy under topnotch control. Before you take steps to calm yourself down after recognizing some signs of a coming danger, determine what kind of anger you are about to express. For instance, if you just witnessed someone being assaulted, you immediately feel a sense of injustice and your brain confirms to you that this is an unhealthy situation that shouldn't be happening. With the sense of injustice comes feelings of anger which can be helpful in the situation. So, in this coming, you don't try to calm yourself or change your emotional state, what you do is use your anger as a motivating factor for doing something to change the situation. Anger sometimes gives us a much- needed courage to stand for a change or initiate one. However, if you sense that the coming anger is one that makes you feel excessive distress and discomfort or makes you want to lash out at something or someone, then you know it is an enemy and you have to prevent it from taking control or consuming you. In this case, you work on the emotion triggering the anger to calm yourself down.

Use effective anger management techniques to calm yourself immediately you sense a pending outburst of anger. Once you become self-aware of your anger warning signs, you can start using some anger management strategies to calm yourself before the storm. It is easier to tame your temper when you are already familiar with your anger triggers and signs. There are different techniques you can try out to help you maintain your cool and keep anger at bay. Here are some strategies you can employ to manage your anger;

- Concentrate on the physical sensations your body gives when anger starts brimming. Although this may seem like counterintuitive techniques, it can be pretty helpful. Focus on your physical sensations by tuning into the very feelings your body gives when you start getting angry; this can reduce the intensity of the anger you feel and alter a possibly instinctual or impulsive reaction

- Take some deep breaths, slowly. A very deep slow breathing exercise can be helpful conter tension in the body. The idea behind a breathing exercise for releasing tension is to take a deep breath right from the stomach, making sure you take in as much air as possible into the lungs.

- Take a quick walk or any other physical activity. When you are faced with an anger-triggering situation, going for a brisk walk can help you avoid expressing the anger the wrong way. Physical activities and exercises help release the built-up energy which otherwise may be used to lash out unhealthily at a person or object nearby. This can really help calm you so you can approach the situation with a cooler version of yourself. For example, if you get in an argument with your spouse and you can feel your anger bridling, simply tune into your emotions and take a walk from the situation so you can calm yourself down. Of course, this may be challenging to do but with resilience and regular practice, you will get better at taking that much-needed walk away from self-destruction.

- Tune into your five senses for quick stress relief to release the tension and knots in your muscles. Your senses of sight, hearing, smell, taste, and touch can all be used to activate immediate stress relief so you can calm your mind and body. You can tune into your senses by stretching the areas of tension, stroking a pet or something dear, listening to your favorite music, or savoring a great cup of coffee.

You can also manage your anger better by devising or finding healthier outlets for releasing pent-up anger. Devising healthier means to express feelings of anger is key to successfully master your anger because like we have said, you aren't meant to hold your anger in. If you think a situation is really unfair, unjust, or wrong, the one thing you can do to change this situation is to find healthier and non-destructive ways of expressing the induced feelings of anger. As long as you have healthier means of expressing your anger, also keep it in mind that you should know when to let go. If you can't agree with a conflict even after expressing your anger, ensure you know when to draw the line and move on from the situation or person who is the source of the anger.

Communicate your feelings with a trusted person. Talking to someone you trust is a great way of easing stress and letting out the feelings you may have bottled in. This person does not need to have answers to your questions or solutions to your problem; simply talking to them can provide instant relief from stress and anger. Communication in this context does not mean venting or lashing out verbally; it is more about talking about your feelings and seeking a fresh and entirely new perspective to whatever situation is on ground. Venting will only reinforce your anger not decrease it.

The last course of action in anger management is to **seek professional help** especially when you know that your anger isn't something you can work on by yourself. There are times when anger management strategies and techniques are simply not enough. In this case, you can go for an anger management class where you can meet people with similar anger problems and learn tips for managing/controlling your anger from trained anger management professional. You can also go for either individual or group therapy to explore the source of your anger and identify the possible triggers. Therapy is a very safe place for expressing all of the emotions you have bottled inside you. It is also a great place to discover new healthy outlets for expressing feelings of anger.

Before you express your anger in any situation, ensure that a calm demeanor is already achieved and you are in the position to approach the problem from a level-headed angle.

CHAPTER FIVE

HOW THE BRAIN IMPACTS YOUR EMOTIONS?

What impacts emotions? This is a valid question to ask if you want to understand and master your emotions. From the context of this chapter, we will be looking at two important things that impact emotions; the brain and social norms/culture.

The brain is a grandmaster in manipulating emotions so even when you think you know the source of your feelings or emotions, it could be really tricky. We like to think we are in control of our feelings and the triggers behind these feelings, but the truth is our brain has a much more profound impact than people like to admit.

Every single moment, there are lots of activities going on in your head and the brain is at the center of all these activities and somewhat complex processes. A lot of processes is involved in how we interpret situations and react to them. Remember that emotions are defined by three important things: cognition, responses, and reaction. The brain determines every one of these activities which makes us wonder how our brain actually impacts our emotions. What happens in your brain right before you experience an emotion?

The first thing to know about your emotions is that it starts right from the brain. Emotions are a combination of our feelings, the way we process these feelings, and our responses or reactions to those feelings. The primary purpose of emotion, according to Charles Darwin, is to encourage seamless human evolution. In order for us to survive, we have to pass on our genetic information from generation to generation which is why emotions are important. Recognizing the importance of emotional experiences, the brain takes it upon itself to evaluate stimuli and activate a suitable emotional response to it. The brain reflects and considers the best way to respond to a situation so that the primary purpose of survival is achieved and then, it activates suitable emotion as response so as to propel the rest of the body to react accordingly. So, when you find yourself reacting to a situation with a kind of response, that is actually your brain triggering the emotion it considers right for your survival right at that moment in time.

The brain is a vast network of complex processes that include information processing. One of the brain's primary network contains neurons which send signals from one part of the brain to the other. Now, these cells or neurons transmit signals through what we call neurotransmitters; some kind of chemicals we either receive or release in the brain. The neurotransmitters are what make it possible for one part of the brain to communicate with another part. Dopamine, norepinephrine, and serotonin are some of the most examined neurotransmitters. Dopamine is the neurotransmitter that has to do with feelings of pleasure and rewards; it is the chemical that makes you happy when you do something good. This neurotransmitter is released as a reward for you to give a pleasurable and happy feeling. On the other hand, serotonin is the neurotransmitter linked with learning and memory. It is believed to play a critical part in brain cell regeneration and research has shown that an imbalance in serotonin can lead to an increase in stress, anger, anxiety, and depression. Norepinephrine on its own help modifies your moods by controlling the levels of stress and anxiety.

Now, when there are an abnormal or unbalanced release and processing of either of these chemicals, there is usually a very profound impact on your emotions and emotional state. For instance, when you do something that requires dopamine to be released and sent to the part of the brain responsible for information processing but your brain doesn't process or receive the dopamine as it should, it could result in you feeling sad or mildly unhappy. Therefore, the abnormal release and processing of dopamine, serotonin, and norepinephrine have immense impact on the emotions you have and the responses you give to certain situations. The next time something which should have made you happy gives feelings of sadness, remember these neurotransmitters.

Again, your brain exerts influence on emotions because it is central to how emotions are formed. The brain consists of different parts that are all responsible for generating different emotions. The part of the brain responsible for processing emotions is the 'emotional brain' which is generally referred to as the limbic system. In this limbic system, we have the amygdala which, as we have said in a previous chapter, helps you measure the emotional quality or value of a stimulus before initiating an appropriate response; it is the part of the brain responsible for initiating the fight or flight response. The hypothalamus helps you regulate your responses or reactions to emotional triggers. There are also other parts of the brain like the hippocampus which all impact your emotions due to its memory retrieval functions. In fact, the hippocampus determines your emotional responses to triggers. Since different parts of the brain process different types of emotions using different methods, damage to any part of the brain can have a huge influence on your emotions and moods no matter how mild. Central to all of this is the limbic system which takes a generalized and simple approach to stimuli.

The brain's left and right hemispheres also play important roles in emotion and responses. The hemispheres are responsible for keeping you functioning but they also play a part in how you process information. The left hemisphere deals more with concrete thinking while the right hemisphere concentrates on abstract thinking. Because they both process information in different ways, the left, and right hemispheres work together to manage emotions. While the right hemisphere identifies an emotion, the left hemisphere interprets the emotion. For instance, when the right part of the brain identifies an emotion like anger, it alerts the left brain which then makes a logical decision in interpreting the context of the emotion and deciding the appropriate response to give. This is actually all a synchronized system but if something goes wrong and one hemisphere can't do its job properly, it affects how you react to basic emotions. For example, if the right brain doesn't identify a negative emotion like it should, it prompts the left brain to become overwhelmed with the emotion without knowing how to respond.

Memory whether long-term or short-term is the function of the brain and our memories dictate and inform our emotions. You get angry when you recall a resentful memory and get happy when you remember a pleasant memory. This is a continual process in the brain; it identifies a past emotion and then places you in a mood based on the emotion. So, when next you get angry without knowing why, it may be your brain recalling some painful memory to initiate a negative emotion. How you can override this is to push yourself to think of things that have made you happy in the past. For example, if you are sad, simply thinking of some happy memories can trigger the release of dopamine which rewards you with feelings of happiness.

HOW CULTURE IMPACTS EMOTIONS

Culture also has a huge role in determining how we perceive, experience, and respond to our emotions. The culture in which you live has laid-down rules, guidelines, expectations, and a structure to help you understand, interpret, and express your emotions within an acceptable context. Based on where you live, there is probably a standard for the accepted degrees of emotional display. Culture dictates how you experience or react to negative emotions; there are guides to help you regulate how you react to emotional triggers. Different cultures appropriate different contexts to different facial expressions and as we have said, there are theories which believe that our facial expressions are cues for the emotions we may be experiencing.

Culture is the values, beliefs, and behaviors that make up the way of life of a set of people and it can also profoundly impact your perception of emotions and reaction to emotions. Cultural display rules influence how you experience emotions by providing rules to regulate your emotions. For example, in European culture and a place like the United Kingdom, individuality is highly promoted while many Asian culture such as China promotes social harmony, not individuality. This means someone from any part of Europe is more likely to express their negative emotions both with others and on their alone while a Chinese is less likely to express their feelings in the presence of others. So, a person from a culture that encourages social harmony is more likely to be the emotion-repressing type because they always try to evaluate the right response which fits the socially acceptable structure and guideline.

Again, every culture has certain consequences ascribed to the expression of different negative emotions. There are cultures where expressing a negative emotion like anger can cause you to be socially ostracized. In the United States of America, a man could be socially ostracized for crying in the presence of others. Cultural norms also impact how both genders perceive and display emotions. Studies in the past have provided evidence to show that men and women may experience and display emotions differently based on some socio-cultural guidelines. Culture also impacts how emotions are interpreted, either by you or the object of your emotion. Cultural contexts influence how we interpret facial expressions of emotions. People who come from different cultures will likely interpret the same facial expression in entirely different ways.

Although our cultural contexts impact how we experience and display emotions universally, emotions are universal because all humans have the ability to recognize and make facial expressions. The seven universal emotions which we will always experience and display no matter our culture are: happiness, sadness, anger, fear, surprise, contempt, and disgust. These emotions have the same meaning across the universe but our culture and cultural display rules will profoundly impact the responses and reactions we give to these emotions either as an individual or a society.

CHAPTER SIX

DEVELOPING EMOTIONAL INTELLIGENCE

Developing emotional intelligence means mastering your own emotions and that of others so you can give appropriate and controlled reactions or responses in stressful or emotional-triggering situations. Emotional quotient refers to how you process emotions so you can make sound decisions. Below are some helpful tips to help you increase your emotional intelligence so you can live a positive, stress-free life.

1. Practice Self-Awareness

As you have learned in previous chapters, self-awareness is an important skill required in emotional intelligence. With emotions, you never win until you know exactly what these emotions are. The lack of self-awareness makes it hard for you to manage your emotions; it is simply like going to sea without a sail, you'll be at the mercy of the currents without being able to control whatever happens. Without self-awareness, you would have no idea what you are doing or where your emotions could lead you.

Practicing self-awareness means understanding your thoughts, perceptions, and behaviors. Know what you are doing, how it makes you feel, and how it doesn't make you feel. Knowing what you are doing starts with getting rid of distractions in your life and engaging your environment so you can know what to tune into and what to tune out of. Silence and solitude are especially critical to your mental health. Find time to get away from things that constitute noise and encourage stress. Distractions contribute a lot to most of the negative emotions that overtake how you feel and act. So, removing distractions is the first step to take before you move on to processing how you feel.

Pay attention to what you feel so you can accurately process these feelings. At first, paying attention to your feelings may seem frightening because of what you may discover. You may come to the realization that you are constantly being a jerk to people around you or they are the ones who are constantly being a jerk to you. You may realize that there is anxiety within. At this point of realization, do not judge yourself or the emotions you are experiencing. All you need to do is be cognizant of these emotions so you can start processing them the right way.

2. Channel your Emotions

A critical skill required for emotional intelligence is the ability to channel your emotions rather than shove them down or force them away. Many people make the mistake of thinking emotions can be "controlled" but you can't control your emotions. In the context, "controlling" your emotions means mastering them and learning the best ways to react to them. Emotions are a part of you meant to inform you when there is something to be attended to. What you can then do after seeing this thing that you need to pay attention to is to recognize whether the thing is important and the appropriate course of action to take i.e. addressing it or not. There are no good or bad emotions; there are only good or bad responses to emotions. Anger becomes 'bad' when you channel it the wrong way and use it to hurt yourself or others. However, it is a 'good' emotion when you channel it to right a wrong or protect yourself from others.

In emotional intelligence, psychologists refer to the ability to channel your emotions appropriately "goal-directed behavior."

Therefore, managing or mastering your emotions is entirely about

channeling the emotions through the right outlet and towards the

right thing.

3. Respond, don't react

In an argument, it is easy to have an emotional outburst and feelings

of anger. But when you are emotionally intelligent, you learn how to

be calm even in the face of a storm. Emotionally intelligent people

are never impulsive even under pressure; they don't react, they

respond after careful and critical examination of the current

situation. In cases of conflicts, the goal is not to argue but to reach a

resolution so, learn to focus on aligning your actions, thoughts, and

emotions with that goal of resolution. This is a conscious effort you

should make to develop your emotional intelligence skills.

4. Listen before responding

In any conversation, ensure you always listen before you respond to

the situation. Emotionally intelligent individuals always wait for

clarity in a conversation before they give a response. This is to

ensure that they understand the context of the situation before they

give a fitting response. However, you shouldn't just listen to the verbal details of the conversation; also pay attention to the nonverbal details being communicated. This helps prevent misunderstandings and ensure accurate interpretation of the message being conveyed. Doing this can help your brain understand the context of the situation or conversation so you don't respond or react in an emotionally inappropriate way.

5. Communicate Assertively

Assertive communication helps you earn respect without demanding it passively or aggressively. Learn to say "no" when needed and "yes" when needed, without explaining yourself or finding excuses; it will help you prevent putting yourself in situations you can't get out of. However, when saying no or yes, ensure you do this with absolute respect. Emotionally intelligent people communicate their thoughts, feelings, perceptions, and emotions in a directly and assertively manner while retaining respect for others.

6. Motivate yourself

Self-motivation is a necessary skill in emotional intelligence and you need it to master your emotions so you can channel it the right way. As an emotionally intelligent person, your actions should motivate you and the people around you. Even when you are facing a challenge that seems frustrating and makes you want to give up, stay resilient and constantly motivate yourself. If you are in a situation that is pushing you to anger, motivate yourself to stay resilient and keep your anger under control.

7. Keep a Positive Attitude

Attitude is a very powerful and important thing in our communications and interactions with others. A negative attitude affects your relationship with others and it can easily infect other people with the negativity. Being self-aware yourself and others help you stay aware of the moods of people so you can dictate their attitude towards you. Emotionally intelligent people know what button to push and what to do; they know how to have a good day and be optimistic. So, practice being positive about your circumstances, situations, and life in general.

8. Handle Criticism well

The ability to handle criticism well is a crucial part of developing and increasing your emotional intelligence. Rather than getting defensive and offended when people have a contrary opinion to yourself, take a moment to understand where the criticism or opinion is coming from. People with high emotional intelligence try to realize how their emotions are affecting their behaviors and performance so they can resolve any issue from a constructive angle.

High emotional intelligence can help you build and maintain great relationships with people; having a good relationship with people around you can have a positive impact on your physical and mental health.

CHAPTER SEVEN

CONTROLLING AND CHANGING YOUR EMOTIONS FROM NEGATIVE TO POSITIVE

Emotions like stress, anxiety, and anger could try to put you in a negative spiral but you can use them to your advantage and transform them from negative to positive. No matter how gloom your life looks right now, you can take charge of your emotions and bring positive vibes and energy only into your life.

If you still remember, we talked about channeling your emotions to the right thing using the right outlet. Negative emotions are highly unwanted because they make us lose touch of the present to live in a miserable, uncertain future. The reason why these unwanted emotions impact our life the way they do is because we haven't learned to channel them in the right direction. Once you learn to channel them rightly, you can easily use them as massive motivating factors to get whatever you need in life.

Firstly, learn to never generalize your emotions and the effects they have. There may be a voice in your head always reminding you that you make so many errors or you don't exactly say the right thing to people in any situation. Of course, you should listen to this voice but you should also remind yourself that this doesn't exactly happen every time. Take a pragmatic approach to every interaction or communication you have with others and always remember that in reality, you will sometimes make mistake and sometimes do the right thing. Being realistic about your emotions is the first key to managing negative emotions using a positive approach.

Being self-compassionate is one way of changing negative emotions to positive. There are times when you have dialogues with your inner self and instill negative thoughts and behaviors. In times like this, turn toward yourself and ask how you would respond if it was a friend. Naturally, you wouldn't be as hard on your friend as you would be on yourself. So, be conscious of when you are being hard on yourself and try to ease up. Make time to engage in some self-pampering activities. Be a very good friend to yourself. Whenever your mind tries to reinforce negative thoughts, remind yourself of self-compassion. Be kind to yourself.

Stop being hasty in making conclusions and reacting to situations. For instance, if you are in a situation that portrays all shades of negativity, do not jump into conclusion about this situation. Instead of doing this, step away from the situation for a moment and try to see the other angles which your emotions may otherwise have blinded you to. Look at it from another perspective, as the emotionally intelligent person you are. Examining a situation for all possible perspective before reacting so you can have a better understanding of the situation and find ways to channel it to achieve positive results. Also, live in the present only and leave all form of uncertainties about the future alone. Living in the past or worrying about what may happen in the future will only fuel your feelings of stress and anxiety and even lead frustration which may trigger anger.

Detect possible negative train of thoughts and bring it to a halt every time you catch yourself. Challenge every form of negative thoughts or feelings trying to sneak its way into your mind or behavior. When a negative thought pops up in your mind, try to find the basis or the proof of it. Doing this will also make you look at the positive sides. The more you do this, the better you become at breaking the pattern of negative emotions and channeling them to something positive.

To begin with, you can channel anxiety and transform it into energy. Anxiety will either make you weak or strengthen you to prepare for what's coming. For instance, right before an examination, you may feel extremely anxious but rather than letting the anxious feelings break you, the right course of action is to channel it to energy and use this energy to prepare for the examination. There are skills you can learn to equip your mind with the power needed to face challenges in life and you can only learn these skills and use them effectively by channeling the power of your anxiety to become a brimming energy level.

Change an emotion like envy to motivation. Envy is a very powerful emotion which humans experience and when you can't channel envy correctly in the right direction, you tend to unfairly criticize others. Unfair criticism of others is one of the surest ways of inviting negativity into your life. Rather than make envy a negative emotion though, you can channel it to become your biggest source of motivation. Do not hate the person you are envious of, make the feelings of envy your ultimate motivating force so that you can have that drive to be successful. If you are unable to do this, an emotion like envy can lead to unnecessary stress, anxiety, anger, depression, and even encourage self-destruction.

Transform your feelings of insecurity which can arise from anxiety into contentment and satisfaction. Like envy, insecurity is a powerful emotion which sometimes stem from anxiety or result into anxiety. Your personal, professional, and relationship problems could put you in an insecure state but you can channel them into ensuring self-contentment and satisfaction. For instance, if you are experiencing financial insecurity, don't let that insecurity project you into becoming worried, anxious, or certain. Instead, take it as a motivation and work hard to change the financial insecurity into absolute contentment. People who feel insecure about money have the biggest chances of becoming millionaires or billionaires. Why? Because they have a motivating factor which is their insecurity.

Anger, stress, and anxiety can be very powerful and motivating emotions, but only if you channel them in the right direction. If you don't find ways to channel these emotions into positive directions, they will break you instead of making you. Remember that an emotion is only negative as long as you approach them as negative.

CHAPTER EIGHT

GETTING RID OF NEGATIVITY IN YOUR LIFE

Negativity and positivity are a constant part of life but negativity has

no-so-healthy effects on us and potentially everyone around us. It sets limits

on our dreams, goals, and aspirations. Negativity can adversely affect how

fulfilling and purposeful our life is. It also has huge effects on our health,

whether physical or mental. Studies have shown over and over that people

who vibe with negative energy are more prone to stress, anxiety, sickness, and

depression than people who are surrounded by positive energy only.

When you make up your mind to rid your life of negativity and start

encouraging positivity and you actually act on this decision, you start to engage in productive things and meet productive people only. Positive experiences sweep away negative energy in your life. One thing to know is that you can't completely get rid of negativity because it is a crucial part of life experiences and human survival; however, you can limit the level of negativity you encourage in your life by doing more of positive behaviors, thoughts, or actions. Below are tips to help you get rid of negativity and enhance positivity.

- **Be Grateful for Everything**

Entitlement is a dangerous thing because it can make you have skewed expectations of people. It is quite easy to start believing you deserve everything you have when life is all rosy for you. This could make you develop a sense of entitlement which causes you to have unrealistic expectation of others and how they should cater to your needs, wants, and everything else. Selfish entitlement is one of the surest ways to set yourself up for a negativity-filled life. People who never appreciate the life they have to a harmonylive in a constant state of lack and discontentment and there is no way to live a life of positivity this way. Becoming grateful and showing appreciation for everything you have in life, from the littlest to the biggest, makes you change your mindset from a place of lack to a place of contentment. Once people notice this new you, it becomes easier to develop harmony in the relationships they share with you. The more grateful you are, the more you receive. This single action can instantaneously make life more positive, fulfilling, and encouraging.

- **Laugh more, even when there is no Cause**

Life can feel draining sometimes due to the many activities going on; tight schedules, busy relationships, work, and everything else. In the midst of all this busyness, it is quite easy to start feeling more like an android rather than a human (no offense to androids). Living with a work-driven, serious mindset will do nothing but bring negative results and performance. It makes you take life so serious that you forget to laugh sometimes. Encouraging positivity means living life with a less serious mindset and giving yourself some break. You only live life once so why burden yourself with all of those responsibilities? Laughter is a great way of reminding yourself that you are human. A laugh brightens your mood and that of people around you; remember laughter is infectious. Laugh more at jokes and stop being so sensitive to light sarcasm. Too much seriousness will only encourage stress. Do not just laugh at people though; laugh more at yourself too. The more you laugh at yourself and the mistakes you make, the more interesting and exciting life becomes.

Happiness is key to positivity so encourage happiness in your life. Remind yourself of happy experiences in the past and laugh your heart out till you are satisfied. Encourage your brain to release more and more dopamine.

- **Change your Perception and Thinking about Life**

You have two choices in life; be your friend or be your enemy. To initiate any change in life, you have to start from within yourself. If you really want to be rid of negativity and become more positive, change your perception of life, situations, and the circumstances you find yourself in. A negative perception of life can be really corrosive so start making active efforts to change your perspectives about life. When you fail a test, do not see it as failure or incapability; instead, see it as an opportunity to work harder and do better.

- **Help others**

Selfishness goes hand-in-hand with negativity just like entitlement. Stop living for yourself only and start living for others too. This isn't to say you should take on the responsibilities of others and leave yours; it is more about creating a balance between how you help yourself and help others. People who live for themselves tend to have no purpose or calling in life. If you live for yourself and no other person, it would be very hard to live a life of purpose and fulfillment. Negativity defies purpose while positivity accompanies fulfillment and purpose. The best way to start creating purpose in life is to help people around you. Helping people can be something as simple as flashing them a bright smile or asking them how their day went. Doing things for others, no matter how little, gives you a sense of value and direction which helps you develop positivity.

- **Spend more time around positive people**

The people we spend time around have a lot of impact on the kind of energy that surrounds us. Sometimes, the negativity in your life may be because of the toxic people you spend time with; they may be friends, colleagues, relatives, or partner. You are likely to become more like the people you spend time around. If your clique is filled with negativity-inclined people and energy vampires, then you are likely to learn their behaviors and become like them. It is almost impossible to live a life of positivity if all the people you spend time with don't even portray positive behaviors. As you rid yourself of negativity and become more positive, you may find that you friends notice the new you and appreciate it or try to convince you that the change is unnecessary.

Change is scary and challenging from afar but once you initiate it, the process becomes a seamless experience. Taking the steps, no matter how small, will help you change your overall perspective and attitude towards life. Once you rid yourself of negativity, life becomes brighter and purposeful.

CHAPTER NINE

HOW EMOTIONAL INTELLIGENCE CAN MAKE YOU MORE PRODUCTIVE

Emotional intelligence can be quite beneficial in making us more productive, purposeful and provide us with a sense of direction. Being emotionally intelligent opens your mind to the abounding opportunities which you can tap into. Emotional intelligence improves the quality of life you lead and helps you create more productive interpersonal and professional relationships. Here are the benefits of emotional intelligence which you should never miss out on; find out how emotional intelligence can make you more productive.

1. Mastering Emotional responses

Emotional intelligence makes you cognizant of your emotions so that you can control the responses you give to situations that trigger these emotions. When you master your emotions and emotional responses, you become less vulnerable to counterproductive reactions and unstable moods. Letting stress, anxiety, and anger control take hold of you makes it difficult to think rationally and this can affect your productivity both at work and everywhere else. When you are emotionally intelligent, you become aware of possible emotional responses and place them under immediate control.

2. Promoting Self-care and stress/anxiety management

Every day, you are faced with one difficult situation or another which requires you to make some really tough decisions. Sometimes, you have to overwork yourself just to achieve more and be productive. However, this can be quite counterproductive to do. Emotional intelligence trains you to recognize your limits and stay within the boundaries of these limits. Being emotionally intelligent means taking a more proactive approach to situations and also taking proactive breaks when necessary. This prevents you from overstressing yourself or having an emotional breakdown which can quite affect your productivity. Emotional intelligent helps you get more done so as to avoid getting burned out or tapping out. An emotionally intelligent person knows working longer hours won't make them more productive so they take a more proactive approach to achieve productivity.

3. Improving Team Collaborations

Emotional intelligence improves your ability to collaborate with others and work in groups. People who are emotionally intelligent are great at collaborating with others and collaborative efforts are usually more productive. Emotional intelligence makes it easy to read, analyze, and process the emotions, strengths, and weaknesses of others and this can help you devise better ways to achieve productive results. Since empathy is a core skill in emotional intelligence, you also find it easier to put yourself in place of others and determine how they might react to a situation. This makes for great adaptability skills i.e. you find it easy to adapt to any environment you find yourself. It also means you find it easier to make logical and required sacrifices for the group which makes your effort even more productive. Good communication, trust, and value always abound in a group where emotionally intelligent people are.

4. Improving Critique-handling ability

Whether harsh, negative, or positive, emotional intelligence help you handle criticism better. The most emotionally intelligent people usually go out of their way to receive feedback and incorporate it to improve the quality of their work or personal relationships. As an emotionally intelligent person, you never stake criticism personally; instead, you make use of every critique to work harder and make an improvement on yourself. As an emotionally intelligent person, if someone says you are prone to anger, you don't explode in their face thereby proving their point; rather, you accept their submission and then look inward to yourself, see if it's true, and make changes to improve. Emotional intelligence also teaches you to give your own feedback to people i.e. if someone does something to wrong you, you make them know immediately instead of keeping it in.

5. Increasing receptivity to change

No one knows change is necessary and required more than an emotionally intelligent individual. Since emotional intelligence enables self-awareness and promotes self-care, it gives you the required tools to initiate change and also deal with any change you find in your way. There is no point in facing change with a negative mindset and this is exactly what you learn with emotional intelligence. Many people tend to welcome change with nasty attitudes and indifference; this makes it impossible for them to initiate or advocate for change even when it is absolutely necessary. Emotional intelligence gives you a positive outlook that helps you welcome change whether it is desired or not. As someone who is emotionally intelligent, you will even encourage others to embrace positivity and inspire yourself to embrace it too. Change, whether personal or social, becomes much easier when you develop and improve your emotional intelligence skills.

6. Building and Maintaining Valuable Relationships

The relationship you have with others should be one that impacts the quality of life you live positively. There is no point having relationships that add nothing to you and this is something all emotionally intelligent people know. People should be in your life because they add value to you and you reciprocate the gesture. Being emotionally intelligent helps you decipher people fast enough to know if they are the type you want in your life or not. However, it is not enough to simply build quality and valuable relationships; you must also strive to maintain the relationship you have built with others. Emotional intelligence provides you with the cognizance you need to maintain your valuable relationships and do away with the toxic ones.

As a person, it is possible to have low emotional intelligence but with practice and consistency, you can develop your emotional intelligence skills. People with low emotional quotient tend to go through tougher challenges than people with high EQ since they have no idea how to manage their emotions or relationship with others. To live a life of direction, it is highly beneficial to learn and embrace every emotional intelligence skill there is.

CHAPTER TEN

MINDFULNESS, VISUALIZATION, GUIDED IMAGERY, AND RELAXATION TECHNIQUES FOR INSTANT RELIEF FROM STRESS, ANXIETY, AND ANGER

Mindfulness meditation, visualization, and guided imagery are all relaxation techniques you can use to keep your calm whenever you feel some turmoil within. So, one by one, let's check out how you can practice each of these techniques for relaxation.

Mindfulness

Mindfulness is a quality inherent in all of us but we don't know how to channel it. Thankfully, experts have developed meditation techniques targeted at helping you achieve mindfulness which is the ability to become so in tune with you, your emotions, and your environment.

- Firstly, find a quiet and calm spot in your home or anywhere else you deem quite enough to fully appreciate nature. This place should be tidy, without any form of clutter. Ensure there are lights on whether natural or electronic. You may also sit outside but make sure there is nothing to distract you.

- Next, assume a sitting position in the right posture. It is important to sit in the right posture so as to ensure concentration and minimal distraction. Find a suitable spot to sit, be it a chair, a bench, or a meditation cushion. The sitting spot should be stable, solid, and stationary. Ensure you are aware of your legs and how they are positioned. If you are on a cushion, place your legs comfortably in a crossed position. If you are on a chair, ensure your feet are touching the bare ground. Sit in a straight position without stiffening your body. Let your arms be positioned in a parallel position to your upper body; your hands should be on the top of your legs. Finally, ensure you lower your eyelids so that your gaze falls slightly downwards. Remain in this sitting position for some seconds and relax your body.

- Focus on your breath and the sensations you feel in your body. As you breathe in and breathe out, feel your breath and focus on the sound. Notice everything from the air leaving your body through the nose or mouth to the air entering the body; the rise and fall of your tummy and chest. Make a mental note of every breath you take, in and out. As you do this, take note that your attention will eventually shift from your breath to other things. Have no worry; mindfulness has nothing to do with the elimination of thoughts. Simply return your attention to your breathing each time you notice your thoughts wander.

- In case you need to adjust your posture or physical position, pause your breath before you do this. Whether it is something as simple as moving your hand or scratching your hair, pause. Ensure you do this with intent, leave a space between what you are currently doing and what you need to do.

- Again, your mind will wander over and over to other things; this is normal. However, do not try to engage these thoughts because they will make you lose your concentration totally. Instead, bring your mind back every time it wanders to something else.

- Do this for about 10 minutes and when you are ready, lift your gaze from the ground and open your eyes if they are closed. For a minute, listen to your environment and notice any sound. Listen to your thoughts and emotions. Now, take a decision and determine how you'd like to spend the rest of your day at that moment.

There, you are done. Mindfulness is just as easy as that although you will find it's not as simple in practice. Concentration is key and it is usually so easy to lose your focus.

Visualization

Over the years, visualization has been used to achieve calm, relaxation, and relief from stress, anxiety, and depression. It is a simple case of using images in your head to project yourself to a place you'd like to be; a place of calm till your body itself becomes calm. Some people even consider visualization to be a form of superpower they can use to achieve anything they want. People often regard visualization and guided imagery to be the same but they aren't. Guided imagery is great for stress relief while visualization is more effective for achieving a set goal. You should too! Here is how to practice visualization.

- Find a comfortable and quiet sitting corner without distractions. Take your seat, close your eyes and prepare yourself to imagine what you'd like. It's just like looking at yourself using a different eye. Note that visualization is best practiced when you just wake up or when you are about to retire to bed. This is when you are most relaxed and when your mind is most free.

- Now, visualize an image of yourself sitting in a movie theater with the lights dimmed. The movie starts and there is an image of you being the best version of yourself on the screen. Include as many details as possible; your clothes, emotion, facial

121

expression, physical movements, the environment, and every other important detail. Try to make yourself experience whatever feelings you think you want to experience in this visualized version of yourself. For example, if you are practicing visualization to reduce your anger; project an image of a much calmer version of yourself.

- Next, stand up, take a walk to the screen, open an imagined door, and enter into the movie of yourself. Now you can live and experience everything from inside yourself. This strengthens the effect of the visualization process. Spend as much time as you need to take in all the details; hear the sound and feel the emotions.

- Once you are done, walk out of the screen which still has that image of you, and return to your theater seat. Sit for a while, then grab the screen and crumple in your hands until only a smaller version remains. Take this in your mouth and swallow it. As you swallow, imagine that is the project better, calm, and well-behaved version of yourself being ingested into every cell and vein in your body. Finally, imagine the ingested screen lighting up your body and feel yourself become a pro at controlling your feelings of anger and handling emotions better.

- Finish up and go about your daily business with an improved mindset.

Make visualization practice a part of your everyday routine and watch as life becomes better.

Guided Imagery

This is a highly effective technique for stress and anxiety management which you can practice every day to relieve yourself of stress and other uncomfortable emotions. It has to do with picturing a person, object, event, or memory that makes you feel calm, relaxed, and happy. To do guided imagery, you have to concentrate on all five senses.

- Find a quiet place without noise or distraction. Close your eyes and deeply breathe in and out to relax your mind.

- Once your mind and body are relaxed, visualize yourself in a calm and tranquil environment of your choice. This place may be imagined or real, from a happy memory. It could be your ideal holiday location. The environment should hold strong, emotional meaning to you.

- Ensure you use all five senses in the visualization of this place. If it is by the sea, hear the rush of the waves and feel the sand. Immerse yourself completely into the environment.

- Now, take your time and relax. Spend as much time as you want in this place, breathing in and out slowly and deeply.

- Once you are done and ready to leave, project your mind back to your current location. You will feel an instant calmness, a holdover your emotions, and a refreshing energy which makes you feel like you can achieve just about anything.

CONCLUSION

Congratulations, you have made it to the end of this delightful read! Mastering your emotions and overcoming negativity may at first thought seem like something that is unachievable or impossible. However, using all the tips and techniques you have learned from this book, you will find it is quite an easy thing to do.

The book has taken you through an in-depth, extensive, and impactful journey on how you can manage stress, anxiety, anger, and develop a mindset fueled by positivity. As promised, you have been made privy to valuable information on how you can rid a life of negativity and get started on the path to productivity, purpose, and positivity. We have checked out all you need to know about stress, anxiety, anger, and the different techniques you can use to manage these emotions. Using everything you have learned from the book, get ready to propel yourself into a positivity-driven, ambitious, purposeful, and stress-free life of ultimate happiness!

www.ingramcontent.com/pod-product-compliance
Lightning Source LLC
Chambersburg PA
CBHW051026030426
42336CB00015B/2736